CAPITAL PUNISHMENT
IN THE BAHAMAS
The Privy Council's Moratorium

CAPITAL PUNISHMENT IN THE BAHAMAS
The Privy Council's Moratorium

by
Dr. Michael D. Toote

authorHOUSE®

AuthorHouse™
1663 Liberty Drive
Bloomington, IN 47403
www.authorhouse.com
Phone: 1-800-839-8640

Published by AuthorHouse   06/18/2013

ISBN: 978-1-4567-9883-3 (sc)
ISBN: 978-1-4567-9884-0 (e)

Library of Congress Control Number: 2011915766

Table of Contents

ABBREVIATIONS

CCJ—Caribbean Court of Justice
IACHR—Inter American Commission on Human Rights
IACHR—Inter American Convention on Human Rights
JCPC—Judicial Committee of the Privy Council
OAS—Organization of American States
UN—United Nations
UNCHR—United Nations Commission on Human Rights

Acknowledgements

This book is the result of a desire to appreciate the dialectic between culture and religion, and politics and the rule of law in commonwealth countries, generally, with particular interest in the Bahamas and the Caribbean, relative to capital punishment.

Acknowledgements are divided into three groups:

- Those whose life work, associations and interactions have kept before me the stories of both the victims of crimes and those convicted and penalized for the crime of murder created the experience and information required to write this book;

- Those who read the manuscript and offered constructive insight resulting in timely corrections involving a subject of a somewhat ever changing and complex nature; and

- Those who honed my potential as a legal scholar and nudged me forward through crucibles of critical thinking in preparation for advocacy in courts of law and civil society.

In the first category, for their contributions to nation building, are Thaddeus A. Toote, my grand uncle and barrister-at-law, and William Thompson, churchman and historian, both deceased.

Also, the book emerges from a culture that is substantially oral in nature which, in far too many cases, is denied valuable insights into what makes it unique in its essence. Persons who can are hard pressed at times to write their stories down for the benefit of society. Ideas and stories that relate to jurisprudence and the rule of law need not be silenced with the demise of those who bear such treasures in earthen vessels. Thus, those who by their relentless enabling, urged upon me the need to undertake the research dealing with capital punishment in light of the Privy Council's moratorium are acknowledged.

The undertaking would not have been completed had it not been for the unconditional support of my wife, Brenda and family who continue by their love and good will to ensure my professional and personal fulfillment. I am forever grateful to my professors at the City University, London, who taught me the art of legal research, namely Allison Wolfgarten and Margo Taylor. Emma Lanlehin helped in my quest to reconcile the relationship between the law as a task master and the need to be gracious in its practice to achieve the highest good for all who make up the mosaic tapestry we have come to know as society. A considerable debt of gratitude is owed Dr. Elliston Rahming, noted criminologist, former superintendent of Her Majesty's Prisons and Bahamas Ambassador to Washington, for his endorsement.

Foreword

The issue of capital punishment—its finality, efficacy and applicability—has exercised the minds of legal scholars and ordinary citizens since time immemorial. In this groundbreaking book, Dr. Michael Toote, a dynamic leader of intellectual thought on matters related to justice and society, treats capital punishment with balance, insight and courage.

Cognizant of law as a dynamic, ever-evolving body of knowledge that connects and cements society in the face of burgeoning social change, this discussion on capital punishment and the posture of the Privy Council is both illuminating and thought provoking.

The decision by the Privy Council to remove the mandatory application of the death penalty as a response to murder convictions and to lay down a discretionary template instead, has become a source of great controversy and has challenged prevailing underpinnings of our culture, politics, religion and jurisprudence throughout the region. Mindful of how the law helps to shape and enhance our understanding of society, Toote manages to skillfully avoid the emotionalism often associated with this subject and takes the reader down a path of scholarly endeavor that leads to a greater understanding of justice in the Bahamas and the wider Caribbean.

Amazingly, he has done all of this with profound clarity and enviable simplicity. Quite clearly, Toote has succeeded topically and thematically at peeling off the layers of legal jargon and slicing off otherwise conflicting, confusing legal precedents in a way that makes this work not just readable, but enjoyable.

In this book, there is truly something for everyone. Indeed, I am impressed by Toote's humane, sensitive approach to a subject that is ordinarily esoteric in content and emotive in intent. Anyone with an interest in contemporary sociology and justice issues-psychologist and cleric; lawyer and enforcer of the law; educator and student; laborer and homemaker, the youth and the elderly-all will find this primer on social thought a must-read as we move from feelings to analysis on critical social questions.

I highly recommend this book to anyone who seeks a proper orientation to criminal law, with particular reference to capital punishment. Take my word—you will find this book to be a most erudite and delightful read.

Elliston Rahming, Ph.D.
Bahamas Ambassador to The United States

Chapter One

Death Sentences and the Privy Council

'The Devil and the Deep Blue Sea'

When one considers the historical summary of death sentence verdicts in The Bahamas in view of the Privy Council's posture, it appears that the jurisdiction is caught, in the words of the old adage, 'between the Devil and the deep blue sea'. Death sentences with reference to Capital Punishment verdicts issuing from homicides in the Bahamas have, for the most part from 1996, not been carried out. A majority of persons sentenced to death by hanging have had their sentences commuted to life in prison. The commutation of death sentences by the Judicial Committee of the Privy Council, also called the 'JCPC', has implications for the rule of law and the aims of justice, namely, certainty, clarity and efficacy of the judiciary.

Restrictions to the death penalty have come from rulings of the Privy Council who, rather than challenging the constitutionality of the death penalty, have ruled that it is not mandatory.[1] This has raised the issue of the Caribbean

---

[1]   M. Shorani, 'A Journey of Two Countries: A Comparative Study of The Death Penalty in Israel and South Africa' (2001) 24 *Hastings International & Contemporary Law Review* at 279-280.

Court of Justice, also referred to as the 'CCJ', replacing the Privy Council to ensure that domestic law is enforced. This said, alternatives to the death penalty, including abolition, have not been seriously considered as they ought.

The term 'Capital punishment', derives from the Latin *capitalis* which means 'of the head.'[2] Beheading has probably been the most popular method of capital punishment over history.[3] It has been regarded by many as in itself inhumane. Over one hundred countries in the world have abolished the death penalty, either *de jure* or *de facto*, exerting pressure on the Bahamas to conform to international human rights conventions.[4]

Worldwide, the rate of abolition has increased with an average of almost four states a year joining the abolitionist movement.[5] On the other hand a minority of countries retain the death penalty with little or no indication of changing. Though it is not clear whether the United States position on the subject is a factor influencing states which retain the death penalty. Caribbean nations, including the Bahamas, continue to sentence murder convicts to death,[6] a matter largely driven by escalating crime.[7]

---

[2] http://www.answers.com/topic/capital-punishment.

[3] Ibid.

[4] *Amnesty International Website(Web.amnesty.org/web.nsf/print/death penaltycountries eng>)*

[5] *M. Shorani, 'A Journey of Two Countries: A Comparative Study of the Death Penalty in Israel and South Africa'(2001) 24 Hastings International & Contemporary Law Review, p.279.*

[6] *David Adams, 'Jamaica to Bring Back Hanging in Drug Crime Fight', TIMES (London), December 4, 2002, p. 17.*

[7] Former Police Prosecutor Warns of Judicial Collapse in the Bahamas' by Larry Smith, *Bahama Journal,* June 22, 2008.

Context

The preceding challenges have limited both the number of death sentences carried out and the powers available to the Bahamas in sending convicted murderers to the gallows. Other issues in the debate involve conflicts between extant jurisprudence and the Constitution, delay, policies of the Executive in capital punishment cases, cultural norms and religious biases, politics and demographics. The subject also touches on constitutional protections such as the entitlement to life, liberty, security of the person and the pursuit of happiness.

Assumptions

A substantial majority, around ninety percent (90%) of the Bahamian population are in favour of capital punishment, [8] perhaps for the same reasons that in some countries substantial minority favour the death penalty. [9] Staunchly entrenched support for capital punishment can partly be understood in attitudinal and cultural terms as part of a law and order syndrome bordering on the parochial. Much support for the death penalty in the Bahamas is found among three basic groups: those who think there should be harsher penalties for offending criminals, those who see the government as ineffective in handling increasing crime, and those who by their demographics are averagely or not at all educated and the devoutly religious. The study contends that endorsement for capital punishment can be better understood as an expressive act where these traits are

---

[8]   'PM Heads of Government Summit Speech', Bahama Journal, July 1, 1999.

[9]   Dick J. Hessing, Jan W. de Keijser, and Henk Elffers, 'Explaining Capital Punishment Support in an Abolitionist Country: The Case of the Netherlands', Law and Human Behaviour, Vol. 27, No. 6, December 2003.

found, suggesting that alternatives to capital punishment ought to be explored.

The stance of the Privy Council fosters a climate of uncertainty and diminished confidence among the judiciary and the executive branches. The status quo contributes, among other things, to a culture of vigilantism and diminution of the rights of the individual and institutions within Bahamian civil society. The notion that the increasing levels of crime could be attributed to the frustration of stakeholders who, at one end are obliged to carry out death sentences upheld by the constitution while at the other end, are prevented from doing so, will be explored.

Constraints

The book seeks to test the foregoing thesis and will be limited chiefly to cases within the Bahamas and rulings of the Privy Council. Human Rights conventions as well as analogous cases adjudicated in a number of states, including the Caribbean, will help to inform the undertaking as they will doubtless impact conclusions in the end.

I have set forth the problem and the scope of the study in chapter one. In chapter two I will seek to demonstrate how culture, politics and demographics inform the debate on capital punishment in the Bahamas. In chapter three I will provide a critique of the major schools of thought regarding deterrence and the death penalty with implications for the Bahamas.

Chapter four will examine the options available to resolve the conflict having regard to an evolving biblical context. The fifth chapter will explain the appeals process together with an assessment of relevant death penalty cases. The part played by international human rights bodies in relation to the moratorium of the death penalty will be the focus of chapter six. Chapter seven will show how several critical factors operate to restrain the enforcement of capital punishment. In chapter eight I will explore the options available to the Bahamas in the context of analogous Caribbean states and the global abolitionist movement. In the final chapter I will sum up the findings of the study, hopefully providing some suggestions going forward.

Chapter Two

Culture, Politics and the Collective Will

'Between a Rock and a Hard Place'

In the main, Bahamians widely support capital punishment for murder so that those who oppose it are in reality swimming against the tide of public opinion. In the Bahamas, the issue is set within a Judaeo Christian context of a closely knit society with a population of about 303,611.[10] Religion as mentioned touches on every aspect of culture and politics, being practiced both devoutly and casually by most. Individuals who dismiss the public view out of hand are doubtless underestimating the cry of the grassroots. The dialectic of culture and religion, therefore, provides valuable insights into the state of capital punishment alongside the death penalty for murder in the Bahamas. Support for the death penalty is aided by a surging murder rate. In 2007, 79 murders were committed resulting in an almost deafening cry for the resumption of hanging, suspended since 2000.[11]

Prior, in 2000 there were 73 murders setting at that time a record for the highest homicides in post independent

---

[10]   *Department of Youth, Ministry of Youth, Bahamas Government, 2008.*

[11]   *'Death Penalty' by Tameka Lundy Bahama Journal, 4ᵗʰ February 2008.*

Bahamas. In 2001 the murder rate dropped to 44 but such a decline would regrettably not be sustained.[12] By mid 2009, 33 murders were reported compared to 35 for the same period in 2007.[13] On the other hand, by mid 2010 there were 47 homicides, an increase of 29 per cent over 2009. Based on this trend, the Bahamas would exceed 100 homicides within one or two years, considering that the murder rate in early December 2010 was the third homicide record in the country in just four years. At the close of December 2010, the homicide rate was 96, the highest figure ever in the Bahamas to that time.[14] At the end of December 2011, the homicide rate was 127, a number which shattered all previous records for murder in the Bahamas.

Pro-Capital Punishment Environment

Religious bodies for the most part are Christian and are perceived by many as being in support of capital punishment. However, the Christian community in the Bahamas differ widely in their views on the subject. Anglican and Catholic churches have publicly opposed death by hanging.[15] The Anglican Bishop, His Grace, Drexel Gomez, for instance favours life imprisonment over the death penalty. [16]So too is Methodism on record as being opposed to capital punishment.[17] Baptists, who account for more than 40

---

[12] *The Nassau Guardian, 'Turnquest:National Security a Priority' by Krystal Rolle, 10ʰ June 2008.*

[13] *The Nassau Guardian,* 'Lifestyles', by Erica Wells, January 13, 2011.

[14] Ibid.

[15] *Catechism of the Catholic Church, Number 2267, Part Three, Section 2, chapter 2 and The Lambeth Conference 1988.*

[16] 'Panel Split on Capital Punishment' by Artesia Davis and Samora St. Rose, April 9, 1996, Nassau Guardian.

[17] *Bahama Journal 'Death Penalty Row Deepens' by Tameka Lundy, 4ʰ February 2008.*

percent of Christians in the Bahamas,[18] have publicly expressed support for capital punishment.[19]

Religion and Politics

It is not clear, however, whether official statements by religious bodies truly reflect the opinions of ordinary individual church members. What seems clear though is that capital punishment is widely supported by the public at large and held up to the public by some as a remedy to escalating crime and, therefore, a deterrent to crime.[20] Some of the most vociferous proponents of this view are religious leaders.[21] In others, capital punishment seem to foster a climate of vigilantism and revenge and nothing short of a circus atmosphere[22]

In this context a number of politicians have expressed support for the death penalty.[23] Too, some politicians, while voicing their pro capital punishment views, point out the importance of fairness and equality for all persons convicted of the crime of murder.[24] Political figures that publicly stand against capital punishment are in the minority. Some of them were once staunch proponents of the death penalty

---

[18] *CIA, The World Fact Book, 19th June 2008.*

[19] *The Bahama Journal 'Religious and Community Leaders On Capital Punishment' by Stephen Gail, 21st January 2006.*

[20] *'Panel Split on Capital Punishment' by Artesia Davis and Samora St. Rose. April 9, 1996, Nassau Guardian.*

[21] 'Capital Punishment in The Bahamas' by Larry Smith, April 12, 2006, *Bahama Pundit.*

[22] 'Reckley Hanged' by Jessica Robertson, March 13, 1996, *The Tribune.*

[23] *'Reinstating Capital Punishment for Convicted Murderers' by Gladstone Thurston. May 7, 1996, Nassau Guardian.*

[24] Ibid.

which they have repudiated since becoming 'enlightened'.[25] Such a response provides some assurance of respect at a certain level for the human rights of the individual which are guaranteed by the Constitution. This could be a hint that the path to abolition, while riddled with obstacles, is not without signs of hope. Whether this support comes from political expediency or personal values is difficult to assess in the context of this study.

It is not uncommon for a political or government figure to express contradictory opinions with regard to the issue of capital punishment. A number of murder convicts might have been spared hangings but the process was driven anyway in favour of public opinion.[26] Hopefully, strikingly different posture at a Latin American and Caribbean Summit, that one day capital punishment will likely be abolished in the Bahamas as in Europe and Latin America, would soon become reality.[27] Again, this demonstrates the difficulty in assessing the true values of politicians against political expediency when it comes to the issue of the death penalty.

Demography and the Death Penalty

Another factor which obliquely contributes to support for the death penalty in the Bahamas is the pandemic of single parent families. In the Bahamas, in any given year, a majority of children, sometimes exceeding 70 per cent, are born to single parents, many of whom are themselves teenagers. Accordingly, an alarming number of young men are for the most part not properly reared or at all socialized. Consequently, they attain adolescence and

---

[25] *'Panel Split on Capital Punishment' by Artesia Davis and Samora St. Rose,* Nassau Guardian.

[26] *'PM: Heads of Government Speech' July 1, 1999 Bahama Journal.*

[27] Ibid.

adulthood without essential tools to cope with the myriad of challenges lurking ahead of them, making them susceptible to criminal behaviour, deviance and a future characterized by social fragmentation and life long dysfunction, which in some cases defy rehabilitation.

In short, a frightening number of young men are being raised without any or any proper parental presence.[28] The notable absence of fathers in the lives of far too many young men constitutes the fuse on the proverbial time bomb too often being lit by the hand of parental delinquency in Bahamian society, causing our youth themselves to either implode or, alternatively, explode upon unsuspecting members of civil society.

Formerly, the Bahamian family was comprised of a centralized figure, known as a role model, around whom individual family members gathered for coherence and hope to withstand the challenges of the present in order to be preserved for the future. This central figure was a significant adult with whom offspring and other young could attach themselves to the family, discover their identity and thrive. This dynamic enabled the proper socialization of the youth within diverse intra cultural milieu throughout the archipelago. Out of this informal system or arrangement flowed provisions of food, shelter, security and a sense of total well being fostering a climate where people felt acceptance rather than alienation.

Currently, the family as a cohesive unit is gravely threatened in light of empirical data. Legal separations, divorces, teenage pregnancy, single parenting and other phenomena of dysfunction within families have become the norm, overtaking the traditional family institution in the nation.

---

[28]   *BBC News, 'Crime in the Bahamas' by John Thompson, Friday, 30th January, 1998.*

Complicating the problem is the absence of the extended family as a support system of value for the single mothers and offspring who have been orphaned due to a myriad of social ills, including communicable diseases and unabated violent homicides.

Far too many women are now giving birth to children they cannot afford or support. Indeed, the scale of this crisis warrants communities, church, civic organizations and governmental institutions to focus their mind and resources on tackling the issues in unprecedented ways. Contributing to malaise is a atrophy mindset stuck in a moralist rut of a past era, clothe in the guise of faith, which, when examined, amounts to nothing more than escapism and an aversion to exercise the intellect to grapple with increasing difficult and uncomfortable issues that we all must face because they simply will not go away. They are here to stay.

The situation is exacerbated by the high divorce rate of around 50 per cent. The family has always set forth as the foundation of any civil society. Children, missing their fathers or significant male role models, have migrated to gangs and other ill advised associations to satisfy their need for affirmation, identity and security. In their view they have been abandoned by father and mother and betrayed by religious, civic and civil leaders put in place to harness them where they are vulnerable to enable their survival. Similarly, these children loathe the fact that their mothers, who should focus on their nurture, are stretched thin, compromised and too distressed by the task of having to be bread winner and nurturer all at once. In other instances, children are entrusted to third parties such as housekeepers and electronic gadgets like the television and virtual games to rear them.

The status quo is one in which children for the most part bring themselves up by their own wits and smarts from the street. This propels the youth into a world or isolation where they are dislocated, fractured, or detached from the vital forces of society which, if properly engaged, can pull them back from the brink of total destruction. Compounding the problem are teenagers mothers who are themselves unaware of the expectations of parenthood. When we unleash these children aforementioned, abandoned, alienated, emotionally and physically handicapped, lacking self esteem, impoverished, denied, deprived and frustrated on society, what do we get? We get escalating unabated homicides and a plethora of crimes against the person and property, threatening both our quality of life and our very existence as a sovereign people.

Moreover, respect for others and regard for the rule of law and order, which should constitute commonly accepted principles embraced by thinking individuals of civil society, has fallen on hard times in our country. Today, values are substituted for the whim and fancy of the moment. One reason for this is that the British influence in the commonwealth has largely been overtaken and replaced by the cultural norms of the United States where the swaggering, gun toting lifestyle of American rap artists are exemplified.[29] The crude and uncivil is held out to all as the example to follow. This nexus between Bahamian culture and the increase in crime will be dealt with later in relation to the question of deterrence and capital punishment.

Drug Culture

Added to the preceding cultural factors underpinning a crime inducing environment are two societal vices which surfaced in the 1970's, namely illegal drugs and domestic

---

[29] Ibid.

violence. This was a time when, as reported in the The Nassau Guardian, 6th February, 1995, 'everyone from street vendor to parliamentarian and government official had his or her hand out for the illicitly gained narco dollar.' I contend that the economic challenges in The Bahamas is the single greatest cause of the drug culture as it exists today; this notwithstanding the many aspects of societal delinquency. In turn, the drug culture urges on the phenomenon of gangs and, ultimately, homicides.

In a way, history is repeating itself. From 1861 to 1865, President Abraham Lincoln ordered a blockade of the ports in the southern United States. This allowed Nassau to use its port for the illegal transhipment of rum and merchandise throughout the region. Before this, life was hard and labour rewards were few for most Bahamians. As a result of the blockade, money was plentiful and fortunes were made over night. However, economic hardship returned at the end of the civil war. During this period, deviance increased drastically in the society as many became slaves to the very product, alcohol, that earlier made them rich through its transhipment. Today, one hundred and fifty-four years later, economic hardship is again responsible for much of the drug culture and deviant behaviour now seen in the inner-city areas of Nassau and the Bahamas. Due to the decline of the drug trade, many are engaged in alternative criminal activities, one of which involves gangs.

It is commonly held that a generation of youth was lost to the drug culture which swept the Bahamas for at least thirty years. Again, this has been facilitated by an acceptance of values commonly associated with inner-city United States gang culture. The Nassau Guardian, 28th July 1994 opined that 'Bahamians are so prone to copy the American way of life. We want to look like the Americans, we want to talk like the Americans, and we act like the Americans. We just about live like the Americans.'

A cursory look suggests a strong connection between illicit drug use and crime in the Bahamas. Sixty percent of first-time offenders before the court appear on drug related crimes. Moreover, up to 80 percent of repeat offenders are drug dealers or drug users. Drug use is also implicated in other forms of violence such as child abuse, spousal abuse and homicide.

Since no society throughout history has ever solved the problem of drug abuse and violence, it is essential that all in society realize that both will be with us for a very long time. The real challenge of this generation of stakeholders is to refocus resources and create new pragmatic strategies that will reduce the demand for drugs and thereby put a dent in escalating crime.

Gang Violence

To state the obvious, the devastation left behind by the drug culture has created an environment within which gang violence is flourishing. Again, the formation of gangs as a fraternity or sorority, mainly for young males, but not excluding females, is an idea imported to the Bahamas from America and, more recently, from our neighbours in the Caribbean. Its genesis was brought on by delinquency in society generally, and the disintegration of the nuclear family in particular. The arrival and widespread use of freebase cocaine caught the Bahamas by surprise and, in fact, preceded the cocaine epidemic in the United States by at least two years. Both societal delinquency and family disintegration have increased as a direct result of the drug culture.

For one to understand gang formation and its activity in The Bahamas, one has to envision the climate of the early to mid-1980s. During this period, cocaine smothered the population of a quarter million people, spread across an archipelago spanning over one hundred thousand square miles of ocean. Let us imagine that in 1983 the average age of the child of a cocaine addict or drug dealer was 7 or 10 years old. Today those same children would be 33 to 36 years of age. These second generation drug affected young adults would now have children or their own, 16 to 20 years of age with prospects of criminal involvement on a generational scale. Doubtless, the pressure placed on the Bahamas by the United States to clean up its act has caused a decline in the glamorous lifestyle associated with drug profiteering.

In my view, two groups have emerged from this decline in drug activity in the Bahamas; drug addicts, currently in their thirties and forties, and young people, mainly adolescent children of drug addicts or delinquent parents. The former contribute to escalating crime by doing whatever it takes to support their drug habit, whereas the latter contribute to an increase in crime by joining gangs and engaging in gang activity, which by its very nature breathes violence, fostering a climate of wanton homicides.

Today there are scores of gangs in the Bahamas with a concentration in New Providence. Interestingly, the causes which feed gangster living, as well as gang related violence in inner-city New Providence, are strikingly similar to those in the United States of America. Some common causes include a sharp decline in the two-parent family, the prevalence of guns, poverty, poor education and drug addiction.

In 1993 a startling 72 percent of all births in the Bahamas were to single females. Meanwhile, many families headed by women have no or no proper parenting. This absence of parental influence for many young people is interpreted as a lack of family, hence a lack of identity. For many youth, this loss of identity inspires gang activity in loyal recruits.

Gang membership gives young people a sense of security with a corporate identity. Concerning gang involvement most recruits do not even think of getting out. The money and security are too good and the alternatives are too few. Yet, despite the stranglehold that many experience in the gangster lifestyle, it is possible, if not probable to get out.

Central to gang involvement and escalating violence is a cry for respect. Accordingly, young people, especially those in gangs, are tire of so-called decent people in society, 'dissing' or disrespecting them. The need to be respected at any cost inevitably leads our youth into violent behaviour. Void of respect from parents and family, and feeling worthless due to lack of jobs, poverty and poor education, many youth organize themselves into an oppositional culture.

Gang activity is directly linked to an increased mortality rate among the youth where homicide is one of the leading causes of death among black youth. As already intimated, part of the solution to gang violence in the Bahamas is the awakening of social institutions such as family, church, community and government agencies, with both a recognition of the problem and as serious attempt at treatment.

Parents can help by steering their children into healthy peer relationships, especially between the ages of 11 and 21 years, the period within which they are most likely to be attracted to or recruited by 'sticky' or delinquent friends. By flooding the inner-city with caregivers and other concerned stakeholders of civil society there will be more opportunities to transfer proper attitudes to youth which, in turn, would serve to counteract learned criminal behaviour.

The government can further enable this plan of constructive intervention by passing legislation that will treat the root cause of crime and violence in our nation, namely illicit drugs and their trafficking, poverty, inadequate education and family dislocation and disintegration.

The drug trade spawned a type of materialism which devalued life introducing the phenomenon of revenge killings to the Bahamas.[30] A breakdown of the 79 murders committed in 2007 in the Bahamas reveal that half were as a result of domestic violence with the remaining 50 per cent attributable to drug trafficking and revenge killings.[31] Perhaps this justifies a review of the judicial procedure with regard to the death penalty as a substantial number of cases to begin with would fall within the category of crimes of passion as opposed to murder which require premeditation or malice aforethought.[32] Therefore, most of the murders committed in 2007 likely involved victims who were in some way mixed up in the circumstances leading to the crime of murder.

Inner-City Context

The city of Nassau, situated on the island of New Providence is the capital of The Bahamas. With a population of nearly 200,000, Nassau is a major tourist and commercial centre of the Caribbean. The scourge of illicit drugs and the prevalence of illegal guns, together with economic hardship, have contributed to violence as way of life among many of the nation's youth.

Death due to violence is a crisis of national proportion in the Bahamas. Accordingly, Nassau's homicide rate per capita

---

[30]   *The Nassau Guardian, 'Nation Sowed Seeds of Crime' by N. Thomas Brown, Monday, 10ᵗʰ December 2007.*

[31]   Ibid.

[32]   *BBC News 'World: Americas Two Executed In Bahamas,' Thursday, October 15, 1998.*

is higher than that of the United States. Further, most of those killed are either from impoverished families or homes that are severely in need of guidance and support.

The problem, then, provides opportunity for stake holders to take stock of the current threat to peace and security in the country in order to avert a social apocalypse or amoral cataclysm which, if left untreated, will likely destroy the legacy of a potentially great nation.

Intervention can make a difference. I was born in the inner-city to parents who, as far back as I can recall, were economically challenged. Notwithstanding this, they were perpetually industrious. After living for ten years in a ghettoized area of Nassau known as 'over-the-hill', my family relocated to an underdeveloped location of New Providence where I and my siblings spent another ten years. The relocation was caused by my parents who, as stake holders, observed the onset of crime and violence and, thus, enabled our survival and proper socialization. Though both communities are now crime and drug infested, the timely action of prudent parents, stakeholders, preserved my life for this moment of critical reflection on the social pathology of our country.

What stood out to me while growing up is what stands out today, the absence of stake holders or the lack of their felt presence in the lives of people most affected by crime, violence and deviance in society. I felt then, as I do now, that actual contact in the context of genuine concern for the economically and socially challenged of our communities could literally mean the difference between success or failure and life or death for thousands in the inner-city.

In my own development, parents, teachers and the wider family nurtured and cared for me, ensuring that I grew into a responsible and civil individual, fully functioning notwithstanding the challenges of living in a post modern secular culture. Today, though, times have changed and many children are left to rear themselves, flailing in unfamiliar, hostile and unforgiving environments. Arguably, this state of affairs greatly contributes to the crime, violence and the escalating homicide rate in the Bahamas. This raises the issue as to whether persons, spawned from such a mitigating set of circumstances and antecedents, should upon conviction of murder; suffer the penalty of death by hanging.

Mitigating Circumstances

At issue, therefore, is whether death by hanging in the interests of justice is best suited as a penalty for murder in the circumstances outlined. This issue was raised by the Judicial Committee of the Privy Council in *Bowe and Another* where it was held that if judges had discretion taking into account mitigating circumstances, individuals hanged for murder probably would not have been executed.[33] Since 1973 about 63 people were under sentence of death for murder in the Bahamas. Of those sentenced 27 were executed while 36 were commuted to life imprisonment.[34]

The view in *Bowe* would undoubtedly cause a reduction of death penalty convictions in the Bahamas where less people have been hanged for murder than those whose convictions were commuted to life in prison, the deadliest year for hanging being 1961 in which six murder convicts were sent to the gallows.[35] However, whether this would

---

[33] *Bowe and Another, P.C. 8March 2006, [2006]1WLR 1623.*

[34] *The Nassau Guardian 'Killers Spared Hanging', 25th March 2006, by La Shonne Outten.*

[35] 'Capital Punishment', December 7, 1998, *The Evening Bahama Journal.*

help to relieve the current tension between the Bahamian judiciary and the Privy Council is yet to be determined.

If in fact there exists the probability of various degrees of culpability making up the crime of murder, ought there not to be a menu of penalties less than death for murder? The research suggests that there ought to be. There is a need for homicides in the Bahamas to be categorized so that it is determined which cases are death penalty eligible; which cases would warrant a person being sentenced to life in prison, and taking into consideration other circumstances in which lesser periods of time would be issued as a penalty for persons convicted of murder. Amendments in the law should include that where a person convicted of murder is sentenced to life imprisonment, such a life sentence should include that person's natural life, without any possibility of entry into civil society whether or not he or she is rehabilitated.

Currently, in the Bahamas there is only one category of murder and judges issue death sentences at their discretion. It is left to ask whether politicians and other stakeholders possess the collective will to urge the debate in this direction, which is the abolition of capital punishment in the Bahamas. In any event, the courts might have been hinting all along their desire to move away from the penalty of death for murder to its virtual abolition.

Constitutional Amendment

The requirement to abolish capital punishment in the Bahamas is a two thirds majority of the electorate or a three quarters majority in Parliament.[36] It is doubtful that this degree of support could be mounted or the

---

[36]   *Bahamas Constitution 1973, Article 54, Chapter V, 'Parliamentary Powers'.*

collective will galvanized in what is presently a pro capital punishment jurisdiction, locally and regionally. But the margin of support required by law to change the status quo is not unattainable. [37] Canada, in 1988 abolished the death penalty for all offences and since then the murder rate has declined steadily.[38]

If, however, the path to abolition is not chosen, the Bahamian Parliament could follow Guyana and Barbados, to *inter alia* enact legislation which will make the Caribbean Court of Justice the final appellate body in criminal matters for the Bahamas while deciding to reserve or not the Judicial Committee of the Privy Council for civil matters.[39]

---

[37]   *The New Black Magazine, 'Rethinking the Death Penalty' by Larry Smith, June 29, 2008).*

[38]   Ibid.

[39]   *Updated Protocol, Caribbean Court of Justice, Caribbean Community Secretariat 17, April 2000.*

Chapter Three

Deterrence and Capital Punishment

'An Ounce of Prevention and a Pound of Cure'

In the context of capital punishment, deterrence refers to the prevention of crimes including murder by means of a sentence of death.[40] The premise of the deterrence theory is based on the idea that the threat of punishment must be sufficiently severe to counter the benefits of pleasures that the criminal would receive from the crime contemplated or executed.[41] To ensure greatest effect, the punishment must be carried out swiftly so that potential offenders would appreciate a clear cause and effect relationship between the felony and the penalty.

Deterrence may be general as in cases where punishment is directed at preventing potential criminals from committing any number of a wide spectrum of crime or specific as in cases where the object of the punishment is to render the convicted criminal incapable of committing further crimes as a result of the punishment prescribed.[42]

---

[40]   http://www.capital punishment.org/thoughts.html

[41]   http://www.enotes.com/does-capital-article//January 9, 2009.

[42]   Ibid.

Empiricism and Deterrence

While it is clear that the death penalty serves as a tool of the state to specifically deter the convicted criminal from ever again committing an offence, it is not clear that it acts as a deterrent generally for persons in society who may commit criminal offences in the future. It is to this issue of whether capital punishment serves as a general deterrent to the crime of murder that the study now turns. It is easier to *answer* this question one way or another than to *prove* one's answer based on the evidence. The difficulty in providing any satisfactory is twofold: divergent views on the subject are held both by academics and practitioners coupled with the fact that even in death penalty countries like the Bahamas, the number of persons executed is small in comparison to those actually sentenced to death.

Justice and social scientists have long contemplated the general deterrent effect of the death penalty as early as the twentieth century. One set of studies compared murder rates in jurisdictions with and without the death penalty, while others compared murder rates of jurisdictions before and after a moratorium or abolition of the death penalty.[43]

Social scientists discovered no significant difference in murder rates in places with and without the death penalty.[44] Empirical data also suggested that homicide rates neither increased after a moratorium or abolition of the death penalty nor decreased after the resumption of the sanction.

---

[43]   *'The Death Penalty'*, by Thorsten Sellin (1959) American Law Institute, Philadelphia, p. 34.

[44]   Ibid.

Comparative Analysis

More recently, comparative studies have come to affirm the thesis that the presence of the death penalty in law and practice has no distinctive effect as a deterrent to the crime of murder.[45] Among the many challenges confronting the argument is the tendency for researchers on the subject of capital punishment to support their own conclusions.[46] What happens often is that unwelcome analysis of a position on the subject by a researcher with an opposing bias will take place creating more divergence on the matter of capital punishment.

This occurred when opponents of the Sellin school of thought, led by Isaac Ehrlich, contended after studying murder rates between 1930 and 1970 in the United States concluded that for every person executed for murder 7 to 8 murders were deterred.[47] Support for Ehrlich's assumption is found in a later study which claims that for every execution, on average, five murders are deterred.[48] Longer waits on death row before execution lessens the deterrence effect of the death penalty.[49] One less incidence of murder is committed for every four and a half month reduction of death row time intimating that legislation to shorten condemned persons' wait on death row will enhance the deterrent effect of the death penalty.[50]

---

[45] 'A Death Penalty Puzzle: The Murky Evidence For and Against Deterrence' by Cass R. Sunstein and Justin Wolfers, June 30, 2008, page A-11, *Washington Post.*

[46] Ibid.

[47] Isaac Ehrlich, *The Deterrent Effect of Capital Punishment: A Question of Life and Death,* 65 Am. Econ. Rev. 397, 415-16(1975).

[48] Joanna Shepherd, 'Murders of Passion, Execution Delays, and the Deterrence of Capital Punishment', *(June 2004) Journal of Legal Studies.*

[49] Ibid.

[50] Ibid.

However, the conclusions drawn both by Ehrlich and Shepherd have been met with great challenge in that they have not been successfully replicated at any appreciable level as in the case of Sellin's which have been replicated time and time again as new data have become available.[51]

The difficulties in replicating assumptions drawn by the Ehrlich School may be due to large number variables of a socio-demographic, legal, and historical nature. Further, Ehrlich's propositions do not factor in the increased availability of guns or even the decline in time in prison for capital offences such as murder. It is in part due to these challenges that conclusions drawn in the Ehrlich school are inconclusive. However, the results of Ehrlich's opponents have also been hotly debated leaving the inference that social science has not succeeded in disproving that capital punishment deters crime.[52]

If deterrence is inconclusive, the prospect of saving innocent lives is not.

Some persons brought up on murder charges are known to commit murder while on bail.[53] The issue then becomes whether to execute and save additional innocent lives through deterrence or whether the state should abolish death by hanging or other means and put innocent lives at risk of becoming victims of murderers whether within or without prison.[54]

---

[51]   William Bailey and Ruth Peterson, (1997) 'Murder, capital punishment, and deterrence: A review of the literature.' In Hugo Bedau, ed., *The Death Penalty In America: Current Controversies*. New York: Oxford University Press.

[52]   Ehrlich & Gibbons, *On the Measurement of the Deterrent Effect of Capital Punishment and the Theory of Deterrence*, 6 J. Legal Stud. 35 (1977). 'Murder Trial Delayed', by Artesia Davis, The Nassau Guardian www. the Nassau guardian. net/ national_local.

[53]   Ehrlich and Gibbons, *Measuring the Deterrence Effect*.

[54]   'D-Day on Death Row', by Ianthia Smith, April, 2006, *The Nassau*

It seems more in the interests of the public and justice to deter murderers from killing twice or at all. It is arguable that if the death penalty were enforced in the case of Forrester Bowe, a murder convict on death row for eight years prior to the Privy Council's ruling on the mandatory death sentence, prison officer Dion Bowles would not have become the second murder victim on record by same offender.[55]

Imprisonment even for life seems incapable of deterring the crime of murder.[56] In the face of inconclusive data the weight is greater for saving additional innocent lives than not. This argument supports the notion that the death penalty has value as a *specific* rather than a *general* deterrent to the crime of murder and, hence, appears to support capital punishment. Other major world jurisdictions such as the United States have long held that capital punishment is a significant deterrent to the crime of murder.[57] In one study capital punishment is reported to have deterred all kinds of murder, even crimes of passion and murders between inmates.[58]

Brutalization Theory

Given the aforementioned reasoning, the proposition for *not* executing would be in cases where the evidence is clear that the death penalty results in the murders of more innocent victims through what is called 'brutalization', the notion that by enforcing the death penalty, potential murderers are becoming real murderers.[59]

Guardian)

[55] Ibid.

[56] http//www1bptbridgeport.edu/-darmri/capital.html

[57] *Gregg v. Georgia 428*, U.S. 153, 185-186 (1976)

[58] Joanna Shepherd, 'Murders of Passion, Execution Delays, and the Deterrence of Capital Punishment', *(June 2004) Journal of Legal Studies.*

[59] http://www.Michigan Law Review.org/archive/104/2/Shepherd

It is not clear whether Brutalization has impacted the increasing murder rates in the Bahamas. Brutalization as a theory suggests that, if in fact capital punishment administered by the state cheapens human life, would be murderers may deem lethal vengeance as a means of resolving conflict where something of high value is perceived to be at stake.[60] Where it is demonstrated, brutalization motivates the murder convict to think that it is correct to kill those who have gravely offended us.[61]

In order for capital punishment to retain its deterrent effect it is necessary for a considerable number of persons, nine in one study, to suffer the penalty of death, before a decrease in the murder rate is observed.[62] Additionally, in order for the deterrent effect to accrue executions had to take place in close succession, unreasonable delay in executions extinguishing any deterrent benefits.[63]

Brutalization, then, in relation to the death penalty cannot be dismissed even where the evidence might suggest a deterrent effect from the enforcement of capital punishment. Further, though cases have been reported of increase incidents of crime immediately following executions, the practical evidence that murders will inevitably increase because of the death penalty is difficult to establish.[64] There are a number of reasons to argue in favour of and against the death penalty, other than deterrence. It is left then to consider the death penalty

---

[60] Ibid.

[61] William J. Bowers & Glenn Pierce, *Deterrence or Brutalization: What is the Effect of Execution?*, 26 Crime & Delinquency 453, 456 (1980).

[62] http://www.MichiganLaw Review.org/archive/104/2/Shepherd.

[63] Ibid.

[64] 'Prison Security in Question', by Erica Wells, January 18, 2006, *The Bahama Journal* 'Does Capital Punishment Deter Crime?' http://www.enotes.com/does-capital-article//print, 1January, 2009.

beyond the notions of deterrence and brutalization in the context of the public's interest. This sets forth the issue of capital punishment and deterrence as a matter of common sense in light of the inconclusive propositions of the foregoing theories.

Common Sense and Deterrence

While for many the empirical methods employed by the social scientists have been inadequate in treating matters surrounding the death penalty, some proponents of capital punishment suggest the argument of common sense which, in effect, says that what people fear most deters them the most.[65] In the face of death by hanging or other means arguably all convicted murderers seek to avoid execution by engaging in the appeal process to either quash or commute their sentences to life. According to those in the Haag School, this is evidence that the death penalty is feared more than a life sentence.

The common sense advocates also contend that even in the face of inconclusive data from the social scientists as to the effectiveness of capital punishment, the death penalty can be said to have prevented *some* murders and deterred some crime.[66] In Haag's view, with regard to the crime of murder, the death penalty constitutes the most ideal form of retribution.[67] Still, the question is whether the degree of deterrence indicated amounts to sufficient reason to justify the administration of capital punishment in death penalty cases as advocates of both the Haag and Ehrlich Schools accept and which those of the Sellin school reject.

---

[65] 'On Deterrence and the Death Penalty' by Ernest van den Haag, www. public. ia state.edu/-cfehr.

[66] Ibid.

[67] Ibid.

It should be noted here that the common sense approach to the death penalty debate does not categorically oppose other views on the issue of capital punishment by its embrace of deterrence as do Ehrlich and Shepherd.[68] Haag's view represents a practical and philosophical compromise between the entrenched views of some who hold the death penalty is either a deterrent to the crime of murder or it is not. Clearly, everyone will not be deterred at all from committing felonies against fellow human beings. In fact, murderers are the people who have not been deterred.

Deterrence, therefore, does not suggest that it will eradicate all or any particular crime, only that there will be a reduction of the incidence of crime. Deterrence seeks to discourage or prevent new entrants into the profession of the crime of murder.[69] The hardened criminal intending to harm another is already aware of the likely consequences of his actions and is unlikely to be deterred when another of his fellows is executed. He has already counted the cost and as a soldier enlisting in an army to fight the enemy, he has contemplated the likelihood that he may be killed. In fact, after war the soldier's experience is often one of surprise and guilt that he was not killed in keeping with his own expectation.

By enforcing capital punishment the common sense advocates intend that the death penalty would deter persons who have not yet enrolled in the profession of criminal activity. In effect, the number of entrants to the profession of murder would decrease due to the high cost of the criminal activity, death by hanging.

---

[68] Joanna Shepherd, 'Murders of Passion, Execution Delays, and the Deterrence of Capital Punishment', *(June 2004) Journal of Legal Studies.*

[69] Obituary: Ernest van den Haag, National Review, April 22, 2002

Common Ground

What concerns both the abolitionists and the proponents of capital punishment is the inordinate delay in carrying out the sentences handed down in murder cases, the former pointing to inhuman treatment, the latter pointing to the weakening of the deterrent effect. For reasons mentioned earlier, it still takes too long for the wheels of justice to properly address the rights of criminals and the public good from conviction to the end of the appeals process. In such cases deterrence may be of little or no value from the offence to the punishment. Delay tends to destroy the 'cause-effect benefit' inherent in the administration of swift justice to deter future crimes and may help to increase criminal activity according to the brutalization theory.[70] I contend that reformation of the appeals process is critical in both determining the deterrent effect of the death penalty and in promoting the aims of justice, two of which are certitude and clarity.

Notwithstanding that abolitionists and death penalty proponents agree some aspects surrounding the capital punishment debate, both groups support or oppose the death penalty for different complex purposes involving emotional, religious and socio-demographic reasons. For its subscribers, the death penalty is linked to public safety, the peaceful enjoyment of one's inalienable right to life, the pursuit of happiness, and the acquisition of property, all of which allow the individual in society access to the all the 'goods' within the commonwealth of his or her domicile. Proponents offer the philosophical argument that the life of any innocent victim that might be spared has greater value than the life of the convicted murderer.[71]

---

[70] http://www.MichiganLaw Review.org/archive/104/2/Shepherd.

[71] Walter Shapiro, 'What Say Should Victims Have?', AskJeeves.com. Internet, 29 April 2000.

On the other hand, for opponents to the death penalty, the issue is one of ethics, civility and morality. They propose other more humane methods of making criminals accountable for their crimes such as life imprisonment without parole, pointing to the fact that most murders are not premeditated but impulsive and, in such instances, the death penalty cannot be said to be a deterrent.

In these cases where there is such a heightened emotional state as in crimes of passion, it is improbable and highly unlikely that a murderer would contemplate the link between his or her actions and some future punishment, namely, the penalty of death. If such a link could not be contemplated then the consequences having regard to the circumstances should be mitigated, in effect sparing the guilty party from the ultimate penalty to life imprisonment.

The Deterrence Effect in Bahamian Context

At issue is how, if at all, the resumption of death by hanging impacts the discussion on capital punishment in the Bahamas. Executions in the Bahamas resumed in 1996 after a 12 year moratorium. The period just before the moratorium began in 1984 suggests no significant difference in the incidence of murders during the moratorium.[72] From 1979-1983 there were 140 murders in the Bahamas compared to 147 from 1984-1988 of the moratorium.[73]

The increase of seven murders during the early years of the moratorium cannot be conclusively attributed to the fact that there were no executions due to the fact that other variables such as domestic violence, the drug culture and the prevalence of illegal gun trafficking have not been treated

---

[72] Royal Bahamas Police Force, '*Detected Crimes-All Bahamas: 1963-2005*'.

[73] Ibid.

in the analysis. If there were a deterrent effect this ought to have been seen at the resumption of capital punishment from 1984 to 2000 during which death warrants were read and executed upon five murder convicts, Reckley, Mckinney, Wood, Mitchell and Higgs. This was not the case as there were 51 murders in 1996, the resumption year, or 11 more than in 1995, the last year of the 12 year moratorium, suggesting that there was no deterrent benefit accruing as a result of the hangings. Moreover, from 1996 to 2000, the resumption period, there were 287 murders on record compared to 241 murders from 2001 to 2005, a decrease of 41.[74]

The last person to be hanged for the crime of murder in the Bahamas was David Mitchell on January 6, 2000. [75] Notably, there were 74 murders recorded for the same year, an increase of 14 from 1999, suggesting perhaps more strongly than ever that the death penalty in the circumstances did not act to deter persons who would commit murder any more than those who would during a period of suspension. Similarly, it would be untenable to suggest that the resumption of hanging caused the increase murder rate as promoted by the brutalization theorists.[76]

It appears from the raw data of murders committed that there is no significant or any general deterrence to the crime of murder from the enforcement of the death penalty in the Bahamas, notwithstanding that there may be a specific deterrence to the commission of crimes in the country. This suggests the probability that persons who commit murder may do so not out of fear of the death penalty being enforced but for some other reasons which exceed the scope of this study.

---

[74] Ibid.

[75] 'To Hang or Not to Hang is the Swinging Question' by Karan Minnis, November 15, 2007, *The Nassau Guardian*.

[76] http://www.MichiganLawreview.org/archive/104/Shepherd

Crime Endemic

The rates of unlawful killings in the Bahamas since 1963 at the instance of internal government as a colony of Great Britain and in 1973 as an Independent nation have gone from 5 in 1963 to 16 in 1973, to 25 in 1983, to 35 in 1993, to 50 in 2003.[77] This steady increase in the crime of murder is troubling and stood at 79 murders for 2007 or 25.73 killings per 100,000 of the population. [78]

Although some take comfort that the rate is not as stark as Jamaica with 1621 murders for 2008 or 57.9 per 100,000 of the population,[79] the incline in the crime of murder for the Bahamas has implications for national security, social cohesion and civil society in such a young democracy where the median age is 27 for males and 29 for females.[80] Recently, there has been a spate of homicides where victims have been killed by a relative.[81] Hopefully, this is unrepresentative of a new phenomenon in a politically and religiously polarizing society where it appears that everybody knows everybody, with a growing number of victims being murdered by family members.[82]

---

[77] *Royal Bahamas Police Force,* 'Reported Crimes—All Bahamas: 1963 to 2005'

[78] 'Crime Council Wants Hanging' by Candia Dames, January 14, 2009, *The Nassau Guardian.*

[79] 'Keeping Death Penalty Will Not Cut Murder Rates', Tuesday, December 2, 2008, *Jamaican Gleaner News.*

[80] 'Crime Rate Up 14 Percent' by Krystel Rolle, October 21, 2008, *The Nassau Guardian.*

[81] 'Man Kills Brother in a Fight', by Rogan Smith, *The Nassau Guardian.*

[82] 'Leslie Miller wants Closure in Son's Murder', by Rogan M. Smith, *The Nassau Guardian.*

The concern for serious crimes, including murder, heightens in comparison to Great Britain, which achieved abolition as early as 1964 and where there were 734 murders in 2007 or 1.08 per 100,000 of the population.[83] Some point to this stark contrast between the high incidence of murder per capita within the Bahamas and the Caribbean and the United Kingdom to promote the argument that the London based Privy Council cannot fully appreciate the public outcry to retain and enforce capital punishment in light of the threat of serious crimes to the stability of civil society in the Caribbean.

Accordingly, advocates of the death penalty see this as sufficient justification for retaining the death penalty, inferring that it is too soon to speak of abolishing capital punishment within the jurisdiction.[84] This argument is not without merit in light of the fact that the incidence of murder in the Bahamas and the Caribbean is considerably above the internationally accepted threshold set at five per 100,000 of the population.[85] The Bahamas exceeds this average by 20 per 100,000 of the population.[86] Jamaica exceeds it by as much as 50 per 100,000 of the population. These statistics pose a considerable challenge to policy makers who should deal with the death penalty in light of the evidence which strongly suggests that capital punishment does not serve as a general albeit specific deterrent to the crime of murder.

---

[83] http://www.capitalpunishmentuk.org/thoughts.html.

[84] 'Hanging by the Vote', Sunday, November 9, 2008, *Jamaican Gleaner News.*

[85] 'Crime Rate Up 14 Percent', by Krystel Rolle, January 15, 2009, *The Nassau Guardian.*

[86] Ibid.

Chapter Four

Retention or Abolition:
Religious Perspectives

'Straddling the Fence'

Causal Links

The high rate of crime in the Bahamas, with a focus on murder, drives the impassioned call for the death penalty,[87] an abatement of which has been blamed for causing increasing crime in general and murders in particular.[88] This is largely the view of the religious in the Bahamas.[89] Impliedly, the death penalty is a deterrent to the crime of murder even though there is no empirical support for this.[90] Murder rates in death penalty states in one study are higher than in those states without the death penalty, in some cases as much as 44 per cent.[91] These uneasy statistics pitch the Bahamas between the proverbial 'rock and a hard place', in that the citizenry seem to have before them two

---

[87] *The Nassau Guardian, 'To Hang or not to Hang' 15th November 2007 by Karan Minnis*

[88] Ibid.

[89] Ibid.

[90] *Death Penalty Information Centre: 'States without the Death Penalty and Murder Rates,' June 27, 2008.*

[91] Ibid.

unsatisfactory options in the circumstances where crime is rampant.

The study will now turn to the source upon which the pro capital punishment religious view is based followed by anti capital punishment biblical passages, extrapolating aspects of extra biblical sources which shed light on the subject. Later in the study, attention will turn to an assessment of the issue of deterrence.

Religious support for capital punishment flows mainly from two sources, namely, the Constitution which declares in its preamble that, *inter alia*, it embodies an abiding respect for Christian values and norms, the rule of law and the supremacy of God.[92] From this, expressly or impliedly, many conclude that the Bahamas is a 'Christian' nation in which the Bible plays a central role in the life and faith of its people.

The Bible and the Constitution

Both the Bible and the Constitution compete for centre stage in Bahamian society. This creative tension, between the constitution and the Bible, has led not a few to interpret aspects of the Constitution and the law as regards the death penalty *by* the Bible. People, including religious practitioners, cite the Bible as being in support of capital punishment.[93] At times specific biblical passages are used to justify the death penalty in a too narrow and often *a* contextual way.

---

[92] The Bahamas Constitutional Commission, *'The Bahamas Constitution: Options for Change,'* p. 4, <u>Commission Secretariat</u>, *Government of the Bahamas Printing Department, Nassau, Bahamas (2003).*

[93] *Bahama Journal 'Religious and Community Leaders on Capital Punishment' by Stephen Gay, 31ˢᵗ January 2006.*

The proponents of capital punishment point to God's sanction of the practice in the Bible as divine instruction to remedy societal ills. Biblically, capital punishment is chiefly dealt with in the Old Testament, specifically in the Pentateuch, the first five books of the Bible, Genesis, Exodus, Leviticus and Numbers, which mandates the use of it for pre meditated murder.

Two verses of scripture are popularly used to uphold support for capital punishment in the Bahamas, starting with Genesis 9:6 which states that 'who ever sheds man's blood, by man shall his blood be shed, for in the image of God man was made.' The instance of this passage is after the *antediluvian* flood where God establishes a New Covenant with his people and reasserts the place of humanity in the cosmos. Here, since God gave humanity dominion over creation, the taking of human life even by animals warrants the justice of God in defence of preserving the humanity within whom He has placed His divine image. This principle is borne out in the words, 'surely, for your life blood I will demand a reckoning; from the hand of every beast I will require it, and from the hand of man. From the hand of every man's brother I will require the life of man'.[94]

Inherently, God places a premium on human life which should be recognized by all creation. Accordingly, the taking of human life is a most extreme act demanding severe punishment. The second passage is found in the book of Exodus which contains a divine order of the Six Commandment prohibiting murder: 'Thou shall not kill'.[95] More accurately, the word 'murder' should be substituted for the word 'kill' to read 'thou shall not murder'.[96]

---

[94] Genesis 9:5.

[95] *Exodus* 20:13.

[96] *Interpreter's Bible 1952; Mercer Dictionary of the Bible; Anchor Bible*

Old Testament Texts

Of the seven Hebrew words that refer to the taking of human life, the word used in the preceding biblical text refers to the most egregious circumstances. Murder in this case represents the wanton killing of the innocent purely for prurient or sadistic purposes.[97] This suggests that there is a biblical presumption of various degrees of culpability as it relates to murder and its remedy.[98] Further, the word used in the sixth commandment is specific with significant implications for the crime committed and represents killing under law which is the specific law which prohibits it.

It may, therefore, be inferred that the sixth commandment would not prohibit the use of the death penalty in the administration of justice. Also, the prohibition did not cover instances of killing in war, suicide or manslaughter. This eliminates the use of the sixth commandment prohibition as an argument against killing by the state.

Further, it should be noted that though the sixth commandment prohibits the taking of another's life by murder, the prohibition does not at this point provide an express penalty for murder. This does not become an enactment until Exodus 21:12-14 where both a prohibition and punishment for murder are clearly stated:

> '*He who strikes a man so that he surely dies shall be put to death. However, if he did not lie in wait, but God delivered him into his hand, then I will appoint a place where he may flee. But if a man acts with premeditation against*

Dictionary 1992.

[97] *The Bible and the Death Penalty: Implications for Criminal Justice Education',* *Scott L. Johnson, Journal of Criminal Justice Education, Vol. 11 No. 1, Spring 2000, p. 18.*

[98] Ibid.

his neighbour, to kill him by treachery you may take him from my altar that he may die.' (Exodus 21:12-14)

Murder in Old Testament Scripture

The above reference is unmistakeable that there is a penalty prescribed for premeditated homicide, death. The same text points out too that there is a distinction between murder and manslaughter, so that the lesser homicide should not fall into the same class as capital crimes. The requirements of premeditation and malice are elements that make out murder deserving of the death penalty as punishment for breach of divine law. Where these elements are not found in an instance where a person has been killed, justice should warrant a penalty other than death.

The Bible very early on also provided guidelines for tempering justice and ensuring equity for offending parties. In Exodus 21:22-25 it states that:

> *'If men fight and hurt a woman with child, so that she gives birth prematurely, yet no harm follows, he shall surely be punished accordingly, as the woman husband imposes on him; and he shall pay as the judges determine. But if any harm follows then you shall give life for life, eye for eye, tooth for tooth, hand for hand, burn for burn, wound for wound, stripe for stripe.'*

At first glance it may seem that the foregoing passage sets out a prima facie case supporting the notion of capital punishment. A closer look, however, indicates just the opposite. Chiefly, what the passage sets out to do is to constrain victims and their advocates and administrators of justice from exceeding their powers purportedly in the interests of justice. Consider, 'How can an eye be just compensation for loss suffered by a victim?' It is therefore clear to see that more than a literal inference is to be drawn from the passage.

The Evolving Biblical Context

The implementation of capital punishment in the Old Testament was due mainly to its apparent value as a deterrent as seen in the words of Deuteronomy 21:21, 'And all the men of his city shall stone him with stones that he die; so shall you put away the evil from your midst, and all Israel shall hear and fear.' To further the deterrent effect believed to be inherent in capital punishment, those responsible for its enforcement were forbidden to those who offended society by committing the heinous crimes of murder, kidnapping and idolatry.

Two forms of capital punishment are mentioned directly in the Bible, namely, Stoning, the more common, which consisted of all the people hurling stones at the condemned person until he or she died after the process of law[99] and Burning which appears as the specified capital punishment for two offences, a man who marries a woman and her daughter and the daughter of a priest who becomes a prostitute.[100] The burning might have more to do with the stigma attached to the crime than the actual crime itself.[101] It should be noted that all three cases in the Pentateuch that deal with burning involve sexual offences. Also, the punishment by burning seems to have preceded Sinaitic legislation.[102]

To heighten the deterrent value of the punishment required as little time as possible between the offence and the punishment with the body of the offending party

---

[99] Leviticus 24:23

[100] Leviticus 20:14 and 21:9.

[101] 'And Joshua said, 'Why have you troubled us? The Lord will trouble you this day.' So all Israel stoned him with stones, and they burned them with fire after they had stoned them with stones.' *Joshua 7:25.*

[102] Genesis 38:24

impaled on a stake and publicly displayed until the setting of sun, at which time it was required to be removed so as not to further defile the land.[103] In the Bible liability for capital crimes were limited to the perpetrator as opposed to transferring liability to his or her family collectively as intimated by some modern day proponents of retributive justice.[104]

The issue of capital punishment was revisited by Talmudic scholars around 200 A.D., signalling a shift in thinking on the subject. From the strict enforcement of the death penalty, Talmudic thinking taught that any Sanhedrin that put a man to death once in 70 years would be seen as bloodthirsty.[105] Other Talmudic rabbi opined that if they were allowed to sit on the Sanhedrin not one person would be executed.[106]

Accordingly, Jewish stakeholders very early on in the history of capital punishment confronted the challenges posed by the death penalty, with regard to morality and efficacy. They embarked on their enlightened journey of rethinking the death penalty based upon biblical principles, the cornerstone of which was the injunction to 'love your neighbour as yourself.'[107] In this context, the condemned criminal becomes the neighbour of everyone's domicile. The effect of this reasoning required the stakeholders in society to elect the most humane death possible for the murderer.[108] The second biblical upon which the Talmud dealt with the administration of the death penalty was in harmony with what obtains when God allows a life to

---

[103]   Deuteronomy 21:23

[104]   Deuteronomy 24:16

[105]   http://www.answers.com/topic/capital-punishment.

[106]   Ibid.

[107]   Leviticus 19:17

[108]   *Kethuboth 37b, Sanhedrin 45a,* TheTalmud.

expire, the breath leaves, a person dies with the effect that the body is left intact.

This thinking led to the injunction that after the administration of the death penalty the body of the offender should be unharmed, abolishing stoning and burning as methods of punishment for capital crimes. Even in cases where execution was earlier authorized it was to be carried out in such a manner as would cause mutilation or separation of the body's extremities.[109]

In order to comply with the new approach, stoning and burning were replaced by pushing the condemned person from a sufficiently high place to ensure instantaneous death, yet from a place low enough to ensure that the body would not be mutilated.[110] Additionally, death sentences could not be passed without collaborating witnesses, thus ruling out circumstantial as well as hearsay evidence. Consequently, where the Bible provides a wide range of offences that were punishable by death, believing the death penalty to be a deterrent, the Talmud and progressive Jewish thought render the administration of the death penalty almost obsolete.

Many contemporary Talmudic scholars view their stand on capital punishment as simply the biblical intention of scripture unfolded.[111] Due to the fact that only the Sanhedrin could pass a sentence of death, the punishment is no longer administered in light of the fact that they are no longer in existence. The State of Israel, on the other hand, while retaining the death penalty for crimes such as treason in time of war and genocide, abolished capital punishment for

---

[109] *Sanhedrin 52*a of the Talmud.

[110] *Sanhedrin 6:4; 45*a, The Talmud.

[111] Http://www.answerw.com//topic/capital-punishment

individual crimes of murder in 1954. To date Israel has just one instance of capital punishment in 1962.[112]

Moreover, many proponents of capital punishment who cite biblical support overlook the fact that offences other than murder called for the penalty of death in the Old Testament economy, *inter alia*, profaning the Sabbath,[113] blasphemy[114] and dishonouring parents, priests and elders.[115] These passages, considered in today's setting, rebut the notion that the Old Testament treatment of the death penalty is relevant in a post modern era.

Further, even though the Old Testament openly prescribes the wide use of the death penalty, the New Testament provides no overt counsel in which Jesus or the New Testament writers endorse capital punishment as penalty or a remedy for murder. There is also, however, no clear rejection of the death penalty as a punishment for murder. It is fair to assume that capital punishment was practiced in the New Testament economy as it was regularly used by the Romans.[116] Paul, the Apostle, adverts to the validity of capital punishment because his statement assumes there are offences worthy of death.

However, just as crimes which warrant capital punishment in the Old Testament were different for the most part from those requiring it by the state in the New Testament, reflecting an evolving civility, so too the abolition movement today likely represents a civilization naturally progressing over time. Most New Testament statements employed today to

---

[112] Adolf Eichmann, convicted of genocide, was put to death by hanging in a Ramleh prison.

[113] *Exodus 35:2, 31:14-15; Numbers 15:32*-36.

[114] *Leviticus 24:11-14;* Exodus *22:20.*

[115] Exodus 21:15; Leviticus 20:9; *Deuteronomy 17:12, 21:18-21.*

[116] cf. Acts 25:10-11.

justify capital punishment by the religious in the Bahamas do not expressly or at all support the death penalty.

Abolition or Retention

Retention of the death penalty raises issues which by their essence unresolved, causes significant philosophical problems. Firstly, in the Bahamas there are no statutory guidelines to account for the various degree of culpability for murder though the death penalty is constitutionally provided for as stated expressly by Anita Allen, Senior Justice of the Supreme Court.[117] Such an absence of enactments as guidelines would itself be sufficient to nullify death sentences in some jurisdictions.[118]

Second, evidence pro or con does not confirm one way or another that the death penalty is effective as a general deterrent a matter to which the study will turn later.

Third, once administered the death penalty is without recall and would forever prevent those cases from being rectified where mistakes within the judicial or criminal system result in the wrong person's life being taken for the crime of murder. In one study it was found that the death penalty was more expensive than life imprisonment, did not deter murder and killed innocent victims.[119] Over 100 persons have been released from prison under penalty of death on grounds of innocence from the mid—1970's with inferring that any number of them might have also been executed.[120]

---

[117] 'The Bahamas Death Penalty Handed Down In Historic Sentencing', http://www.handsoffcain. info/archivio_news/200604.php.

[118] *Furman v. Georgia 408 U.S. 238 (1972)* United States Supreme Court Case.

[119] 'New Jersey Abolishes Death Penalty,' *National Public Radio*, December 17, 2007. NPR.org.

[120] 'New Suspect Charged in Brewer Case', by John Mott Coffey, Friday,

For this reason alone executions in the United States are at a 30 year low.[121]

Fourth, the administration of the death penalty appears to lack equity in that those who are in general subjected to it are poor, uneducated minorities.[122] Even though no studies have conclusively uncovered a strong racial bias, the cumulative effect of data clearly suggests that the death penalty is imposed at a higher rate on those who blacks who murder than on whites who commit the same crime of murder.[123]

Sixth, death by hanging dehumanises the individual and in its administration cannot be said to be civil. Survival of the sentenced during hanging is between eight to thirteen minutes after which death takes place by suffocation because of a slipknot placed around the neck with a support at the other end. The weight of the body suspended in mid air juts forward, resting on the slipknot compressing the respiratory tract. At times as a result of the hanging, the person becomes cyanotic with their eyes bulging out of the head, the tongue elongated protrudes outside the mouth. Additionally, a groove is left in the neck evidenced by lesions on the vertebrates and internal fractures.

In light of these realities, whether to retain or abolish the death penalty should given be greater national focus moving the public to seriously consider its future quality of life as moral, ethical and rational members of civil society. Why then is the death penalty so attractive to persons of faith or religion in the Bahamas? There is no clear answer

---

February 8, 2008, *Commercial Dispatch Bureau.*

[121] 'New Jersey Abolishes Death Penalty', *National Public Radio*, December 17, 2007.

[122] http://www.answers.com/topic/capital-punishment.

[123] http://www.answers.com/topic/capital-punishment.

in the absence of empirical data. This notwithstanding, socio-demography, politics and attitudes toward criminal justice help shape support for capital punishment, as they also do in staunchly abolitionist countries.[124]

In some societies where there are deeply religious people such as in the Middle East, the United States of America and the Caribbean support for capital punishment appears to be entrenched. Yet, Israel which is deeply religious has managed to abolish the penalty of death for murder. The contrast between Israel's attitude to capital punishment and retentionist jurisdictions may lie in the level of exposure or depth in contemplating the issue over time, intimating that education may play a pivotal role in how an individual or a state may view the topic.

Christian Mindset

The Bahamas is heavily Christianized with many fundamental religious bodies which are guided largely by a literal interpretation of the Bible. Some of these entities function at the extreme end of civil society looking with disdain upon any challenge to religious practice in a post modern era. Rising out of this environment is widespread concern that the government of the day is not effective in handling crime.[125] It is felt by some, including religious leaders, that what is needed is a revised penal code which calls for harsher penalties for offences.

---

[124] *Dick J. Hessing, Jan W. de Keijser and Henk Elffers, 'Explaining Capital Punishment Support in an Abolitionist Country: The Case of The Netherlands' Law and Human Behaviour, Vol. 27, No. 6 (December 2003), p. 605-622.*

[125] *Ianthia Smith, 'Crime Wave Concerns All', Nassau Guardian, March 25, 2006.*

Anyone who thinks that a mere revision of the penal code would diminish or seriously treat the problem of crime in the Bahamas is misguidedly naïve at best and delusional at worse. Crime, regrettably, occurs naturally in any society, helping to make society what it is. It is doubtless the Puritan roots of Western Christianity which lead many religious in the Bahamas to adopt a role in which they have purportedly been divinely commissioned to eradicate evil in the world, including crime, in order to restore the purity and simplicity of primitive Christianity.

The incidence and extreme acts of criminality may, in fact, serve a meaningful purpose even in healthy societies. For instance, when we hear of callous forms of deviance, mainly in instances of homicide, people are overtly expressive and upset. Their anger and disapproval of criminal acts draw them together in ways that are unlikely to be achieved otherwise. Thus, the deviant conduct of one or a few often clarifies the values of the many or majority in society. In so doing values are clarified and respect for human life is demonstrated. At the same time the offender is forced to contemplate his of her own deviance and attending penalty in light of rules which govern civil society.

Crime, then, serves the purpose of bringing people from disparate social strata to fuse together into a common understanding of what constitutes morality and decency in a democracy. The collective experience of these episodes of deviance tightens the bond of solidarity for the benefit of all in society. When we acknowledge that no one is out of reach as regards deviance in the world, solidarity in society becomes a real possibility. However, there is no attempt here at justifying deviance or criminality in society, simply to acknowledge its presence as a fact that cannot be dismissed but, instead, must be reckoned with.

Abolition and the New Testament

Religious leaders, comfortable with the Old Testament dispensation of 'an eye for an eye and a tooth for a tooth' ought to revisit the new economy brought into being by Jesus, who dealt with the capital punishment case of the woman caught in adultery.[126] Jesus summed up his arguments to the pro-capital punishment crowd by two statements, which amount in the first instance to an indictment and in the second to an acquittal or pardon, namely, 'he that is without sin among you, let him cast the first stone'[127] and to the accused 'neither do I condemn you; go and sin no more'.[128]

In effect, Jesus remitted the death sentence of the woman convicted of adultery upon penalty of death to probation on her own recognisance. By his manner and words, then, the Founder of the Christian religion ushered in a dispensation of redemption, forgiveness and compassion, with which the Talmudic tradition complies.

Socio-demographic Context

Although untested, support for the death penalty in the Bahamas might also be related to the fact that, as an Independent nation, the Bahamas has just 35 years of full governance with 50 percent of the population below the age of 45 years of age and is by any measurement still a very young nation.[129] The older population is deeply religious and, by this attribute, are overwhelmingly in support of capital punishment. Many youth and, by extension, persons within

---

[126] John 8:7-11.

[127] John 8:7

[128] John 8:11

[129] *The Bahamas, The World Fact Book. Central Intelligence,USA 19June 2008.*

the adult population are poorly educated as evidenced by a recent national assessment.[130] Where similar results are found strong support for capital punishment have been known to exist.[131]

The way forward, then, should contemplate abolition both as an option to capital punishment and as an indicator of a progressive civil society in a global village. This would entail a sustainable plan of action intent on informing and educating the religious majority in particular and the Bahamas in general as to the issues surrounding the subject of capital punishment. Indeed, it is ripe to consider amending the laws with respect to the death penalty so as to provide for degrees of culpability for the crime of murder especially in light of recent Privy Council rulings which, in effect, strongly caution against death penalty convictions since they can not be carried out without serious legal challenges.

I believe that, notwithstanding the Bahamas' pro capital punishment climate, more needs to be done by the international community, in particular abolitionist countries such as the United Kingdom, to provide strategies and a package of incentives to nudge the Bahamas toward abolition as was offered in other cases.[132]

Incentives for Abolitionists

The power of incentives to affect desired outcomes was seen in Lithuania where the number of murders rose from

---

[130] Tamara McKenzie. 'National Mean Grade.' Nassau Guardian, August 30, 2003.

[131] Hessing et al, 'Explaining Capital Punishment Support in an Abolitionist Country'.

[132] P. Hodgekinson and A. Rutherford, (eds) 1996 'Capital Punishment in Global Perspective' Winchester Waterside Press; British Journal of Criminology (2005) 45(3), 402-406.

224 to 242 from 1990-1996 resulting in a loss of support for the abolition of capital punishment from 27 to 18.3 per cent.[133] Despite this, abolition was achieved in 1998 all because politicians had to choose between pro capital punishment constituents and the national interests of the state, which was offered, inter alia, economic benefits of membership in the European Union.

What could be of help in a campaign toward abolition is ground work which will elicit insightful analysis as to the real thinking of the public regarding the topic. It may well be discovered that the public in the end is not resigned in their support of the death penalty or, alternatively, opposed to the idea of its abolition. A campaign to inform the elites as well as the masses of anti capital punishment arguments should be undertaken with a clear objective of showing why the state, in light of human rights guarantees, does not have the right to execute its citizens.

The campaign to abolition should flag the attitudes of citizens regarding the death penalty as a litmus test to their nation's democratic maturity and willingness to rid them of the extant inhumane system of punishment. Paradoxically, it seems that the principles of democracy lean towards a policy of abolition while defenders of the death penalty support it purportedly on behalf of public opinion.

Moreover, what is needed is courage by the Executive and the administrators of justice collectively focusing the nation's resources, chiefly, human capital on the subject. A part of the process involves causing the electorate to be enlightened on the topic of capital punishment and the option of abolition. Best endeavours should be exerted to study how countries with pro death penalty views achieved abolition.[134]

---

[133] Ibid.

[134] P. Hodgekinson and A. Rutherford, eds. (1996), 'Capital Punishment

Courage and political will should lead stakeholders to take the next step of building coalitions or networks of support with such entities as the church, the media and all political parties. In one instance where such an undertaking ensued, all death sentences were commuted to life imprisonment, murders decreased and the government, sponsoring the initiative, was re-elected for a consecutive term of office. Additionally, and in keeping with building coalitions, social reformists, as opposed to traditionalists and fundamentalists should be nurtured and nudged into office both in the religious and political arenas to achieve the agenda of abolition.[135]

The reality is that, notwithstanding the merits of abolition, capital punishment is constitutionally protected in Caribbean states so that, given the pro death penalty climate, executions will likely continue into the future. Where carried out, it can only be hoped that death penalty states within the Caribbean will consider making the event as quick, painless, dignified resulting in as little disfigurement to the person as possible. There are hopeful signs that the Bahamas will not pursue the death penalty as it has in the past. Effectively, corporal punishment in the Bahamas has been repealed.[136]

Law reform should extend to the matter of the death penalty including its suspension or abolition or both, as the prospect of continued hangings to provide a deterrent to rising crime, including murder, is nothing more than wishful thinking in the absence of adequate tools for the proper prosecution of criminal activity in the Bahamas.

---

in Global Perspective'.

[135] P. Hodgekinson and A. Rutherford (eds.) 1996 'Capital Punishment in Global Perspective'.

[136] 'Corporal Law in the Bahamas to be Repealed', by Erica Wells, November 8, 2008, *The Nassau Guardian*.

[137] This suggests that the risk of mistakes in hanging the wrong person is too irreversible to ever be corrected and is, thus, out of step with equity, civility and justice in a nation which boasts of itself as being Christian.

Finally, The Bahamas as a Christian nation founded on biblical ideals ought to explore a more humane approach of treating persons convicted of murder, calling overwhelmingly for them to suffer death by hanging. One should consider that there is no call for death by the state for the crime of murder in the New Testament and even the Old Testament set rules of due process to ensure that in a case of murder the scales of justice were balanced. Moreover, extra-biblical religious scholars as early as 200 A.D. denounced capital punishment, raising the standard so high that it was almost impossible to enforce.

The life of Christianity's leader, Jesus Christ, set up his kingdom on principles of compassion and forgiveness by which his followers are challenged to live by and dispense to their most heinous enemy, who according to the teachings of Christianity is our neighbour, even the person under sentence of death. Some to whom capital punishment is administered have been known not to die instantly but to linger with contortions of agony before dying. There needs to be then, in relation to capital punishment in the Bahamas, both a deepening of Christian principles as well as a proper understanding of what human dignity requires of every person in civil society.

---

[137] 'Boyd to Uphold Church's Stand on Homosexuality', by Krystel Rolle, January 1, 2009, *The Nassau Guardian*

Chapter Five

Death Penalty Cases and the Appeals Process from 1990-2000

'A Stitch in Time Saves Nine'

Resumption of Hanging

From 1996 to date there have been five (5) hangings for murder in the Commonwealth of the Bahamas. Prior, there was a twelve year suspension of capital punishment (1984-1996),[138] which makes the resumption of hanging from 1996 to 2000 of special significance. The Bahamas has hanged 50 people, all males, since 1929; five under the Ingraham administration and 13 under Pindling, yielding 32 between 1929 and 1967.[139] Since 1973 sixteen (16) people have been executed for murder in The Bahamas. [140]

Two persons, namely, Alexander Barr and Charles Glinton, were hanged during the Pindling administration but prior to Independence.[141] If the judge were allowed discretion as argued by Counsel for the Appellants in *Bowe* and

---

Guardian Ref

Hands off Cain, 1ˢᵗ January 2008

Times, March 9, 2006, Frances Gibb).

'Capital Punishment', December 7, 1998, The Evening Bahama Journal.

Davis both men would probably have been spared the death penalty.[142] The question of why hangings resumed after a 12 year hiatus will be considered later as hangings have done little to curb increasing levels of crime in the Bahamas. [143]

The Appeals Process

Persons under a sentence of death have a general right of appeal in respect of Supreme Court rulings.[144] Internally, the appeals process involves at least four stages. First, upon a conviction of murder the defence files a notice of appeal or alternatively applies for leave to appeal. Second, the Registrar will arrange either for a hearing of the application of the appeal. Third, the defence must show all justifiable grounds on which the appeal is made. Fourth, the Registrar in turn obtains and lays before the Court of Appeal, in the Bahamas, in proper form all documents, exhibits and other things which appear necessary for the proper determination of the appeal or the application.[145]

The Prosecution must inform the court of their intention to appeal following a ruling or request an adjournment to consider whether to appeal. If an adjournment is granted the Prosecution must inform the court following the adjournment that they wish to appeal a ruling. [146]Further to a ruling of the Bahamas Court of Appeal, respondents

---

[142] *Bahama Journal, Murderers Still Awaiting Review of Death Sentences, 3rd June, 2008).*

[143] *Hands off Cain,* above.

[144] P.J. Richardson (ed) *'Archbold: Criminal Pleading, Evidence and Practice,'* Sweet & Maxwell: Thompson Reuters, U.K. (2009), chapter 7-248, p. 1187.

[145] Ibid.

[146] *'Archbold: Criminal Pleading, Evidence and Practice',* chap. 7-194,p. 1161

may proceed with an appeal against the internal ruling to the Judicial Committee of the Privy Council in London.

In contrast, a petition to international human rights bodies such as the Inter American Commission on Human Rights can only be made after appeals have been exhausted at the domestic level. *Article 46(b)* of the Convention provides that a petition must be in a timely manner within six months from the date on which the complaining party was notified of final judgement at the domestic level. This suggests that an appeal may be at the Privy Council while a petition is pending before an international human rights body on the same matter.

Where a judgement has not been issued on a domestic level occasioning a breach of a murder convict's human rights, *Article 38* of the commission provides that the 'dead line for presentation' of a petition shall be within a reasonable time, from the date on which the alleged violation of rights occurred, considering the circumstances of each specific case. Although the Inter American Commission on Human Rights has not set a specific time for hearing of petitions, recent cases by the Caribbean Court of Justice have recommended eighteen months to two years for appeals to international human rights bodies.[147] Where a petition is substantially the same as one pending before another international body, the IACHR will consider it duplicative and, thus, inadmissible under *Article 46(c)* and *47 (d)* of its convention.[148]

---

[147] Amnesty International, January 6, 2000.

[148] This refers to an organization which is competent to take decisions on the specific facts set forth in the situation and measures in favour of the effecting settlement of the dispute concerned. See IACHR, *Reso. 33/88, Case 9786* (Peru), in *OEA/Ser. L/V/II, 76*, Dec. 10, 18, September 1989, pertaining to d-h.

Reckley and Mckinney Cases

First, consideration will be given to the case of Thomas Reckley which was historic, in that, it created a firestorm around human rights, Bahamian juris prudence and the appellate process. Reckley, convicted of murder and sentenced to death under Bahamian law, petitioned for leave to appeal against a refusal by the Court of Appeal of the Bahamas to grant a stay of execution until determination of whether the punishment contravened his constitutional rights.

Mainly, Reckley brought constitutional proceedings on a claim that he was denied the right to see material before the Advisory Committee on the Prerogative of Mercy which was required to consider his case before the Minister advising the Governor General under Article 92 of the Constitution. [149] Reckley's petition was dismissed and after a flurry of other attempts at appeal, via international human rights bodies, Reckley was executed 13th of March 1996, the first such person so to be since 1984.[150]

Departing from an earlier ruling, that some aspects of the prerogative of mercy might be subject to judicial review, [151] it was held that a condemned man did not have the right to have disclosed to him the material placed before the Governor General's advisory committee by the Minister.[152]The second person to be executed for murder after the 12 year hiatus was Dwayne McKinney who met his fate at the gallows on 28th March 1996.

---

[149] [1996] A.C. 527; [1996] 2WLR 281; Times, February 6, 1996).

[150] Guardian ref

[151] Council of Civil Service Unions v Minister for Civil Service (E.H.R.L.R. 156)

[152] Times, February 6, 1996

Fisher's Case

Trevor Fisher followed Mckinney to the gallows, sentenced to death March 1994 for the murder of Durventon Daniels in 1990. After dismissal of appeals under International Law, on 7th June 1996 a petition was filed on his behalf to the *IACHR*, seeking redress.[153] On 5th May 1998, the *IACHR* determined Fisher's petition admissible and scheduled his case for consideration at its session from 28th September 16th October 1998. Meanwhile, the *JCPC*, the Bahamas highest appeals court in London, ruled on 5th October 1998 in response to a warrant issued for Fisher's execution, by a majority of 3 to 2, that it was not unreasonable for the government to schedule his execution as his petition was pending before the *IACHR* for 21 months.[154]

Fisher argued that to execute him while his petition was outstanding would infringe his right to life under *Article 16* of the Constitution and amount to inhumane treatment under *Article 17*. Their Lordships reasoned that there was no express provision in *Article 16* imputing a right to life pending a determination of a petition to the *OAS*, since the Bahamas was not a member of the *OAS* at the time the Constitution of the Bahamas was enacted.[155] In effect such right could not be implied.

Wood's Case

Richard Woods, the fourth person to be hanged since 1984 would have his fate predicated on the *ratio* in Fisher's case. Woods was convicted and sentenced to death in January 1995 for the 'hit and run' murder in 1993 of his niece Pauline

---

[153]   Inter American Committee on Human Rights, 5th May 1998:OAS Website.

[154]   PC 1998, 5th October [1999]2 WLR 349; [2000] 1A.C. 434)

[155]   Ibid.

Johnson. Both men were hanged, notwithstanding petitions pending before the *IACHR*, on 15th October 1998.[156]

Mitchell and Higgs Cases

David Mitchell, the fifth person sentenced to death was hanged on 6th January 2000.[157] A six person convicted of murder, John Higgs, sentenced to death in 1995 for the murder of his wife, Joan Higgs, succeeded in taking his own life on 4th January 2000 while under suicide watch shortly before his scheduled execution. [158] Higgs was retried in August 1996, and again sentenced to death. David Mitchell was convicted of the 1994 murder of tourists Horst and Traude Henning, and sentenced to death in November that year. The *IACHR* wrote to the government one day before the executions stating it would issue a ruling on the cases within two weeks. Sealing the fate of the men, the Privy Council on 14th December 1999 by a 3 to 2 majority said that it would not be unconstitutional to carry out the executions, since more than 18 months had elapsed from filing of appeals with international human rights bodies and that prison conditions for those under sentence of death did not amount to cruel and unusual treatment.[159]

A Synopsis

In the cases of Reckley and McKinney it was held that the operations of the Advisory Committee on the Prerogative of Mercy were not justiciable. However, this reasoning is no longer reliable as in *Lewis* it was held that convicted murderers can now view papers and argue their reasons

---

[156] Amnesty International, 6th January 2000.

[157] Ibid

[158] Amnesty International, 6th March 2000.

[159] Ibid.

for commutation.[160] In Fisher and Woods there was no express provision within the constitution that imputes a right to life under a sentence of death pending a petition to international human rights bodies. Arguably, delay on the part of the *IACHR* to hear and give its decision in a timely fashion worked against Higgs and Mitchell, enabling their executions.

Commutations

Unlike the five persons who were hanged from 1996 to 2000 in the Bahamas, five (5) persons also had their death sentences commuted to life imprisonment beginning in 1996, namely, Dwight Henfield, Ricardo Farrington, Forrester Bowe, Trono Davis, and Larry Jones. The case of Henfield succeeded in further testing the familiar argument that undue delay in carrying out sentences of death amounted to cruel and inhuman punishment contrary to *Article 17(1)* of the Constitution of the Commonwealth of the Bahamas.[161]

Henfield and Farrington Cases

Henfield was convicted of murder and sentenced to death in 1988.[162] The Court of Appeal of the Bahamas dismissed his appeal against conviction and a warrant was read for his execution. In 1989 he was granted a stay of execution pending an appeal to the *JCPC*. By then a number of other condemned men had begun proceedings challenging the legality of the death penalty in the Bahamas.[163] In 1993 Henfield filed his petition for leave to appeal which was

---

[160] *Neville Lewis and Others v Attorney General of Jamaica [2000] 3WLR 178).*

[161] Henfield PC Ref

[162] Reference

[163] Reference

dismissed by the *JCPC*. In 1995 he applied to the Supreme Court of the Bahamas by Originating Motion that the time for which he awaited execution amounted to such a delay as to constitute inhuman punishment under the Constitution.[164]

Amid of the legal controversy, the table turned for Henfield when the Supreme Court granted his Declaration under *Article 17(1)*. Even though the Bahamas Court of Appeal reversed the judge's decision, holding that the five year delay caused by legal challenges to the death penalty should not be considered in determining whether the delay was constitutional, the *JCPC* ruled otherwise.[165]

According to the Privy Council, which allowed the appeals of Henfield and Farrington sentenced to death in 1992, the period for appeals against murder in the Bahamas was two (2) years, so that a lapse of three (3) and a half following sentence of death would be so prolonged as to render execution inhuman punishment contrary to *Article 17(1)* of the Constitution. [166]

Technically, the ruling allows the Court to depart from this time frame although it does not clearly state what would constitute an appropriate departure and on what grounds. However, the Privy Council saw no legitimate basis for increasing the period of appeals when proceedings were prolonged by a failure of the relevant authorities to take steps to curtail the delay.[167] In short, the Council's ruling could be seen as a means to curb unnecessary delays in the justice system.

---

[164] Ibid

[165] *Privy Council* ruling to overturn Bahamas Court of Appeal decision in Henfield's case.

[166] *Privy Council, 14October 1996 [1996]3 W.L.R. 1079 [1997]A.C.413).*

[167] Ibid.

Farrington's appeal against conviction was dismissed by the Court of Appeal of the Bahamas in 1994 and in 1996 the Judicial Committee of the Privy Council dismissed his application for special leave to appeal against that decision.[168] The Advisory Committee then considered his case and advised that the law should take its course. A warrant for his execution was read but in April 1996 he petitioned the Supreme Court that his execution would be contrary to *Article 17(1)* and sought a stay of execution pending determination of his claim. His application was dismissed on grounds that his appeal was bound to fail.[169] Farrington then appealed to the *JCPC* which granted leave ruling that a refusal to grant a stay of execution by the Bahamas Appeals Court was adverse to Farrington's constitutional motion.[170]

In the circumstances, both condemned persons as well as relevant Ministers of justice would have inadvertently or otherwise contributed either by default or omission to cause sentences of death to be commuted to life in the Commonwealth of the Bahamas, further enabling a moratorium on capital punishment at home and abroad.

Bowe and Davis Cases

In the cases of Bowe and Davis, the issue of the constitutionality of the death sentence as mandatory was raised and determined. Both Appellants had been convicted of murder and sentenced to death pursuant to *Section 312* of the Penal Code of the Bahamas.[171] Their appeals against conviction were unsuccessful.[172] They therefore petitioned the *JCPC* to

---

[168]   Ibid.

[169]   Ibid.

[170]   [1997]A.C. 413

[171]   Penal Code, Statute Laws of the Bahamas.

[172]   *Bowe and Another v. The Queen* 8th March 2006 [2006] 1W.L.R. 1623

challenge the requirement of *Section 312* that sentence must be passed on adults, except 'pregnant women' convicted of murder.[173]

The *JCPC* ruled that the Bahamas Court of Appeal's decision be set aside and remitted for reconsideration of the sentencing question.[174] The Court of Appeal held that it had no jurisdiction to entertain an appeal against a mandatory sentence in criminal proceedings and that under *Article 28* of the Constitution any challenge to the Constitution of the mandatory sentence must be made to the Supreme Court. In Considering the conduct of the Bahamas Appeal Court, the *JCPC* held that the Court of Appeal had erred in construing *Article 28* as precluding it from entertaining a challenge to the Constitution of a sentence on appeal, thus, reversing the Court of Appeal's decision[175].

The historic ruling of the Privy Council on Bowe's case meant that Section 312 of the Penal Code should be construed as imposing a discretionary and not a mandatory sentence of death on murder convicts.[176] So construed, it was continued under the 1973 Constitution. This legal epiphany effectively quashed the death sentences of the Appellants and remitted the question of sentencing to the Supreme Court to be determined case by case

The ruling in Bowe was similar to a decision delivered 11th January 2006 of an earlier case in which Lord Bingham, in a densely reasoned judgement concluded that as early as 1973; the mandatory death penalty should have been regarded as an inhuman and degrading punishment. [177]

---

[173] Ibid.

[174] Ibid.

[175] *Bowe and Another v The Queen 8March 2006 [2006]1 WLR 1623.*

[176] *Ibid.*

[177] *The State v. Brad Boyce* (Privy Council Appeal No. 51 of 2004).

Discretion and Law

The ruling in Bowe, spawned a legal earthquake which would send shock waves throughout the Bahamas' judicial system touching all persons in prison under sentence of death. To state the obvious, it came as a surprise both to the lawyers and the public that the mandatory sentence of death for murder was unconstitutional. If it is found to be unconstitutional now it must have been unconstitutional since 1973 at Independence.

What, then, hid this new light from the enlightened all along? According the Privy Council a lack of understanding of the guarantees of entrenched human rights lent to the dark understanding of jurists when dispensing justice in death penalty cases. In their Lordships minds, it is not that the meaning of human rights changed from the 1973 constitution but that constitutional tenets and human rights jurisprudence were unfamiliar to jurists who, along with the court, resisted an appreciation for them.

The significance of the ruling is that the mandatory sentence of death for the crime of murder in the Bahamas is forever abolished, rendering it unconstitutional.[178] This raises a question as to whether even a discretionary sentence of death for murder would long stand in light of legal challenges. By its ruling the Privy Council declared that the crime of murder should be seen as embracing a wide range of varying criminal culpability so that not every convicted murderer deserves to die.[179] Accordingly, persons sentenced to death prior to the ruling in Bowe and Davis must effectively have their cases remitted to the supreme

---

[178] *The Bahama Journal 12th March 2004, 'Murderers Still Awaiting Review of Death Sentences' by Candia Dames*

[179] Foulkes, *Bahamas Journal.*

court for re-sentencing, a process which has not yet been completed. [180]

It is doubtful that best efforts are being made in a timely manner to review death sentence cases affected by the ruling in Bowe even though some cases have been brought for re-sentencing. In one such case, Wesley Giste, convicted of the murder of Oswald Brown, the *JCPC* dismissed the Defendant's appeal against conviction but quashed his sentence of death, remitting the matter to the Supreme Court for re-sentencing in accordance with their earlier decision that the mandatory death sentence in the Bahamas was unconstitutional. Accordingly, Giste was re-sentenced to an additional ten years in prison, having had already served nine years for the same crime.[181]

The ruling in *Bowe* would have the same effect on the Bahamas as the Eastern Caribbean Court of Appeal ruling in 2001 had on St. Lucia, St. Kitts and Belize.[182] In the latter case, it was held that the automatic imposition of the death penalty without judicial discretion amounts to cruel and inhuman punishment.[183] This was the first time a Caribbean state declared the mandatory death penalty unconstitutional.[184] The ruling became judicial precedent when it was subsequently upheld by the Privy Council.[185]

---

[180] *'Prime Minister: Case Could Answer Capital Punishment Question'*, by Candia Dames, *Bahama Journal*, 8th *May 2008*.

[181] 'Ten More Years For Murder' by Tosheena Robinson-Blair, December 4, 2007, *The Bahama Journal*.

[182] *Privy Council to Rule on Death Penalty'*, Tuesday, March 23, 2004, Caribbean Net News

[183] *Spence and Hughes v The Queen*, Criminal Appeal, Nos. 20 [1998] & 14 [1997], (Judgment given 2 April 2001) (Eastern Caribbean))

[184] Ibid.

[185] Ibid.

Discretion Revived

The ruling in *Bowe* means that for the foreseeable future, the procedure by which the death penalty is imposed by the Court in the Bahamas would forever be altered. To be fair, however, the principle adverted to by the Privy Council in its land mark ruling, that the death penalty is discretionary and not mandatory, as some are apt to point out, has always been acknowledged by the courts in that, since 1973, more persons convicted of murder have had their convictions commuted than the number of persons that have been executed.[186]

Degrees of Culpability

By its recent ruling on death penalty issues the *JCPC* may be urging the Bahamas to focus its jurisprudence on the wide range of culpability concerning the crime of murder. Murder covers at one end of the spectrum the sadistic murder of a child for purposes of deviant sexual gratification and atrocities caused by terrorism resulting in multiple murdered victims, tantamount to contract killings. At the other end, murder covers euthanasia of a significant other suffering unbearable pain from resulting terminal disease or a taking of life which results from a real albeit exaggerated or perceived threat of death or grievous bodily harm to one's person, property or family.[187] Varying scenarios of killings which satisfy the definition of murder are not equally heinous or involve the same levels of culpability. Parliament could be of assistance to judges by enacting legislation which takes into consideration various degrees of propensity in the crime of murder.[188]

---

[186] *'Privy Council Rules on Bahamas Death Penalty Issues'* by Sir Arthur Foulkes, May 12, 2006, Bahama Pundit.

[187] Judicial Committee of the Privy Council *Obiter Dicta.*

[188] *Hands Off Cain Website, 'The Death Penalty Handed Down in Historic*

Effect of Discretionary Ruling

It is left now to address the question of discretion as it relates to death sentences in the Bahamas. The ruling of the JCPC in *Bowe* and *Davis*[189] on 8th March 2006 was applied for the first time, one month later, on April 20, 2006 when, in an historic judgement, Senior Justice Anita Allen sentenced convicted murderer Maxo Tido to death for the 2002 murder of 16 year old Donnell Conover.[190] Tido was convicted of murdering Connover on March 20, 2006, twelve days after the Privy Council's ruling that the mandatory death sentence in the Bahamas was unconstitutional.

After considering equally the aggravating and mitigating factors and weighing specified objectives of sentencing, the Judge held that the appropriate penalty in this instance was sentence of death. Since this first instance of discretion, two more men, Ernest Lockhart and Cordell Farrington, were sentenced to death for the murders of Claxton Smith and Jamaal Rollins, respectively.[191] At first Tido's case was said to be 'uncertain' as his appeal was pending before the Courts.[192]Since then, the Bahamas Court of Appeal has upheld the sentence of death passed on Tido by the Supreme Court.[193] Notwithstanding the Court of Appeal's ruling to uphold Tido's death sentence, the Privy Council

---

Sentencing In The Bahamas.' 2008.

[189] [2006]WLR 1623.

[190] Ibid.

[191] Hands off Cain Website,'The Death Penalty Handed Down in Historic Sentence' (2008).

[192] Remarks on 'Swift Justice' by The Honourable Allyson Maynard-Gibson, Attorney General and Minister of Legal Affairs at a Press Conference, Wednesday, May 17, 2006.

[193] 'Court of Appeal Upholds Tido Death Sentence', by Artesia Davis, Friday, October 17, 2008, *The Nassau Guardian.*

in June 2011 quashed the sentence of death in his case, stating that though it was a dreadful murder, it did not fall within the category of 'worst of the worst' and therefore the death penalty should not apply.

It should be noted here that though the sentence of death as a penalty for murder is still constitutional in the Bahamas, the discretionary nature of sentences based on the preceding rulings amounts to the removal of an essential pillar upon which capital punishment stood in the Bahamas for well over fifty (50) years. The death sentence is expressly provided for in *Article 16(1)* of the Bahamian Constitution.[194] Any interference with that provision short of a constitutional amendment would contribute to further legal uncertainty, throwing the court into disarray, making the machinery of justice of little or no effect.

Complicating the issue, the discretionary death penalty means that judges must now exercise their conscience based upon the law in capital cases. According to Lord Bingham, this means that the Court must apply and interpret the Constitution of the Bahamas by ensuring that the rights of convicted persons are protected and that the duties of the courts are at the same time performed in keeping with equity, justice and regard for the rule of law. [195] Added to this challenge is the fact that no judge relishes the notion that his or her discretion in a case could determine whether a person lived or died. Adding to the problem is the absence of any statutory guidelines for providing a menu of equitable sentences for persons upon a conviction for murder.[196]

---

[194] Constitution of The Bahamas (1973).

[195] *'Never Before in the History of England: Privy Council Sits Outside Britain'*, by Clifford Bishop, The Bahamas Investor, Vol. 2, July-December 2007, p. 93

[196] 'The Death Penalty Handed Down in Historic Sentencing in The Bahamas' *Hands Off Cain* (2008).

Notwithstanding these challenges, the Executive continues to pursue the enforcement of the death penalty [197].

Activist and Conservative Judges

Underpinning the debate on capital punishment are contrasting views of the Privy Council and the Bahamian Judiciary, between activist jurists in London and constructionist jurists in the Bahamas. By literally interpreting the Constitution, jurists in the Bahamian jurists mainly adjudicate upon the premise that the Constitution, which is supreme, ought to be conservatively read and applied. This reasoning would doubtless favour and perhaps foster a capital punishment climate, in that the law expressly provides for death by hanging for the crime of murder. On the other hand, the activist stance of the *JCPC* arguably fosters an abolitionist climate considering their rulings of the past ten years. Permeating all this is politics, local, regional and global.

Despite the strong pro capital punishment sentiment in the Bahamas and the Caribbean, the global climate is considerably in support of abolition. In North America, both Canada and Mexico have abolished the death penalty.[198] South American nations have in most cases abolished capital punishment retaining it in some countries only for exceptional circumstances.[199] There are hints that the local judiciary might be adjusting themselves on the question of capital punishment in the Bahamas in favour of the Privy Council's landmark decision that it is not mandatory.[200]

---

[197] '*PM: Case Could Answer Capital Punishment Question*', *Bahama Journal*, 8th *May 2000*.

[198] Amnesty International reference

[199] Inter American Human Rights Report May 2006.

[200] 'God Alone Can Enforce the Death Penalty', by Artesia Brown, November 12, 2008, *The Nassau Guardian*.

This view of change was seen in the remark of the President of the Bahamas Court of Appeal, who in summing up a death penalty re-sentencing case opined *obiter dicta* that only God has authority to carry out the penalty of death. [201] It is yet to be seen whether such a remark is a sign of the times signalling a reformation of thought regarding future capital punishment cases and the Court.

Enlightening Discretion

Every nation in Western Europe has abolished capital punishment as a prerequisite to membership in the European Union, tying governance to economic prosperity and sovereignty, a policy which is fully supported by the *JCPC*, in particular their Lordships Scott and Bingham who have written at large on the impact of legal decisions on the economy.[202] The abolitionist movement has even found support in conservative Africa where Namibia, Angola, Mozambique and South Africa have abolished the death penalty.[203] Conceivably, the Bahamas by supporting the death penalty might only serve to further isolate itself from the international community.[204] The global community has for the most part, in over one hundred nations, either abolished altogether or restricted the use of capital punishment, signalling abolition.[205]

---

[201] Ibid.

[202] 'Privy Council Sits Outside Britain', *The Bahamas Investor,* Vol. 2, p. 93.

[203] P. Hodgekinson and A. Rutherford, (eds.) 1996 'Capital Punishment in Global Perspective', Winchester Waterside Press; *British Journal of Criminology (2005) 45(3), 405.*

[204] 'Capital Punishment in The Bahamas' by Larry Smith, March 15, 2006, *Bahama Journal.*

[205] UN General Assembly, 18th December 2007, Resolution GA/10678 at the 62nd Plenary Session called on states to 'Progressively restrict

Chapter Six

The Constitution and Human Rights Conventions

'The Last Straw'

This area addresses the inevitable dilemma facing both the Jury and the Justices in their roles as judges of fact and law and interpreters of the Constitution, in light of the recent Privy Council rulings on the constitutionality of the death penalty in capital cases in the Bahamas.

Inherent Conflicts

A number of international conventions on the rights of the individual have been seen to be at odds with the provisions of the Bahamian Constitution, which allows for the sentence of death by hanging for murder as one of the punishments which may be inflicted by a court of law within the jurisdiction.[206] However, even though there has been a call by the United Nations for countries to abolish the death penalty, capital punishment remains legal under international law.[207]

---

the use of the death penalty and reduce the number of offences for which it may be imposed.'

[206] The penal code, chapter 84, Title VIII para. 115 (1) Statute Laws of the Bahamas.

[207] UN High Commission on Human Rights report 1999/61 of 58th

Inhuman Treatment *vs.* Capital Punishment

Notwithstanding the right of the courts to apply the penalty of death for murder on conviction, international human rights organizations have responded by pointing to instances of inhuman treatment of convicts as justifiable grounds to spare them from the death sentence. [208]

At the heart of the controversy, then, is what constitutes inhuman treatment. According to *Article 17(1)* of the Constitution no person should be subjected to torture or to inhuman or degrading treatment or punishment. The question arises as to whether capital punishment would be within this prohibitive category of inhuman and degrading punishment. Although this matter will be considered later, *Article 16* of *Chapter III* suggests that where due process has been carried out the person convicted of murder is not protected by this prohibition.[209] The key provision of *Article 16(1)* is that no one shall be 'deprived intentionally' of his life except in the execution of the sentence of a court in respect of a criminal offence of which he has been convicted.[210]

Articles 17(2) and *30 (1)* comprise savings clauses which provide a constitutional safeguard upholding the legality of the death penalty. They provide that nothing done under the authority of any law shall be held to be inconsistent with or

---

meeting on 28 April 1999.

[208] cf. Chaper III, section 15(1) on the Protection of the Right to Life of the Individual, Bahamas Constitution (1973).

[209] *The Bahamas Constitution (1973), Chapter III*, 'The Protection of the Fundamental Rights and Freedoms of the Individual', Article 16(1).'

[210] *The Bahamas Constitution (1973)*, 'Protection of Life' under 'The Protection of the Fundamental Rights and Freedoms of the Individual', Chapter III, Article 16(1).

in contravention of the constitution to the extent that the law in question authorizes the infliction of any description of punishment that was lawful in the Bahamas Islands immediately before Independence on 10th July 1973.[211]

One may infer from *Article 17(1)* and *(2)* that since Capital Punishment was, among other penalties, lawful *before* Independence, it is lawful *after* Independence and justiciable in the current global abolitionist climate. In this lies an inherent conflict where, on the one hand, the Constitution frowns upon inhuman and degrading treatment of the individual while, on the other hand, it provides for the deprivation of life by means of death for the crime of murder.

Set against this constitutional paradox, *Article 4* of the Inter American Convention of Human Rights (*hereinafter referred to as the 'IACHR'*) recognizes the right to life and restricts the application of the death penalty, contending that the right to life is inherent and cannot be suspended for any reason. [212] Where implemented, the clear effect of *Article IV* would be the abolition of the death penalty within the Organisation of American States (*hereinafter referred as the 'OAS'*), including the Caribbean, of which the Bahamas happens to be a member state.[213]

Pratt and Morgan

In *Pratt and Morgan*, Jamaican cases, conflicts were found between *Article 16 (1)* and *17(2)* of the Constitution, which arguably provides legal cover for capital punishment,[214]

---

[211]   *The Bahamas Constitution,* 'Enforcement of Rights,' Chapter III, *Article 30(1).*

[212]   Office of Protocol, OAS Web @ oas.org May22, 2008.

[213]   Ibid.

[214]   Privy Council (Ja) 02 November 1993; Times, November 4, 1993

and *Article 4* of the Inter American Convention of Human Rights, which restricts the imposition of the death sentence in all circumstances, as the right to life cannot be suspended for any reason. In this case two murder convicts were held on death row for eight years.[215]

The Jamaican Court of Appeal withheld its written ruling dismissing their appeal to the Judicial Committee of the Privy Council for about four more years. On the merits, the Inter American Commission on Human Rights heard the case, ruling that in the circumstances Jamaican conduct amounted to inhumane and degrading treatment of those convicted contrary to *Article 5 (2)* of the Inter American Convention on Human Rights.[216] A review of all the facts moved the Judicial Committee of the Privy Council to rule that the 12 year delay constituted cruel and inhumane treatment. Consequently, any delay of more than five years would be so considered, commuting death sentences to life in prison.

Pratt Effect and Swift Justice

Doubtless the Pratt case propelled Caribbean states to process death penalty cases on a timelier basis so as to avoid the debacle of delay which threatened to sink the region in a legal quagmire. *Pratt* in Jamaica was the forerunner to *Reckley* in the Bahamas.[217] Both highlighted tensions between domestic law and the *JCPC* with respect to the death penalty.[218] Additionally, *Reckley* and *Pratt* would also reveal extant tensions between international human rights

---

215 Inter American Commission On Human Rights Website 2008

216 Ibid.

217 *Reckley v The Minister of Public Safety and Immigration (No 2)[1996]A.C. (No. 2)1996.*

218 [1996] A.C. (No. 2)1996

bodies and constitutions of Caribbean states in general and the Bahamas in particular.

Reckley was convicted of murder and sentenced to death after exhausting his appeals four and a half years after sentencing. The Privy Council, dismissing an appeal that *Reckley* should see materials placed before the advisory council on the prerogative of mercy regarding the sentence, upheld the decision of the Bahamas Courts. Attempting to wiggle out of this legal dilemma with the five year period about to expire, the Bahamas proceeded to carry out the death sentence notwithstanding an appeal to the human rights commission of the Organization of American States.

The question was whether the Bahamas breached its obligations to the *OAS* as a member state. This does not appear to be the case as the Bahamas, though a member of the *OAS*, [219] is not yet a signatory to the Inter-American Human Rights Commission which comprises 25 countries, mainly within Latin America.[220] This arrangement may help to ease tensions between the Bahamas and the Organization of American States of which the Inter American Commission on Human Rights is a part. However, the conflicts between laws of Caribbean states and the IACHR will not go away anytime soon.

Both *Pratt* and *Reckley* signal a growing trend within Caribbean jurisdictions, that international human rights bodies are seen as wielding more and more influence among jurists, regional courts and the Privy Council. It

---

[219]   Organization American States Website@oas.org 2008; all 35 independent countries of the Americas have signed on as members. Cuba is excluded from participation in the OAS by resolution of Council of Foreign Ministers in 1962.

[220]   Inter American Commission on Human Rights Website: @cidhoea. oas.org.

should be noted however that this influence is persuasive, not legally binding. Subtly, though, by its persuasive voice, international human rights bodies seem to be scoring moral victories in the campaign to abolish the death penalty. The United Nations resolution, 104 to 54 with 29 abstentions, calling for a moratorium on the death penalty is another blow to the practice of capital punishment.[221] The effect of the resolution means that world opinion is against capital punishment so that practicing states are increasingly becoming more and more isolated in the juris prudential global village.

Effect on Judges

What then should judges who are bound to apply the law of the land do in death penalty cases? Should they simply go through the motions of trials and appeals of death sentence cases only to wait on the Privy Council's predictable ruling or should they take an activist stance and legislate from the bench?

These are relevant questions in light of the Privy Council's willingness to take note of death sentence appeals to international human rights bodies. Both in *Pratt* and *Reckley*, the Privy Council agreed that human rights institutions had standing to hear death penalty petitions. In this the Privy Council might signal that Courts within death penalty jurisdictions should consider prevailing world views against capital punishment and take such views into their juris prudence.

Perhaps this is what the Judicial Committee of the Privy Council intended when, in *Bowe and Another v. The Queen*, [222] it ruled that the sentence of death was not mandatory

---

[221] UN General Assembly Report at 62nd General Assembly Meeting, 18th December 2007, GA/10678.

[222] *8 March [2006] 1WLR1623.*

but discretionary.[223] On the other hand, some jurists may see this ruling as creating more uncertainty in an already uneasy legal situation. For instance, it shifts the burden of determining verdicts from the jury to judges, in the process diminishing a pillar of the jury system of trial by one's own peers. Which judge properly formed would honestly relish the thought that his or her ruling would determine the irreversible fate of a convicted murderer? Not many or any. Further, it is improbable that a judge would be classified as peer of a convicted murderer.

Notwithstanding the above mentioned challenges, one potential benefit from the Judicial Committee of the Privy Council's ruling abolishing the mandatory death penalty is a wider range of possible sentences for the crime of murder. This would afford judges greater latitude to contemplate all the circumstances and possible sentences before determining a penalty for murder.

Need for Reform

However, there is a need for greater compatibility between the provisions of the Bahamas constitution and the rulings of the Privy Council and international human rights conventions regarding the death penalty. Title 20, *Section 291* of the Bahamas penal code provides that 'whoever commits murder shall be liable to suffer death'. Death is defined by *Title 20, Section 290* as 'the intention to cause death of another by unlawful harm'.[224] What is needed is a mechanism which will require relevant human rights clauses to have *Direct Effect* upon member states rather than mere persuasive authority. A course of dealing by subscribers

---

[223] The JCPC in 2001 confirmed the ruling by the Eastern Caribean Court of Appeal (2001).

[224] Title 20, Section 290, Penal Code of the Commonwealth of the Bahamas.

to the United Convention of Human Rights and the Inter American Convention of Human Rights which complies with the spirit of the respective conventions would also be helpful in providing much needed clarity in expediting death penalty cases appeals.

Constitutionality of Death Penalty

Clearly, the death penalty in the Bahamas is constitutional as all challenges to its legality have failed. This was the ruling handed down by the Judicial Committee of the Privy Council on 3rd April 1995 in *Larry Jones v The Attorney General of the Commonwealth of the Bahamas 1995*.[225] Technically, the proceedings ended on 11th April 1995 when Her Majesty in Council approved the Board's judgement on the date formerly stated.[226] If the Larry Jones proceedings had been successful they would have meant that the carrying out of the death penalty in The Bahamas was unlawful.[227]

The effect of this ruling in favour of the death sentence is mitigated by *Article 90* of the Constitution which confers on the Governor-General a power of pardon. *Article 91* and *92* establish an Advisory Committee on the Prerogative of Mercy (*'The Advisory Committee'*).[228] Where an offender has been sentenced to death the relevant Minister is bound to cause a written report of the case from the trial judge together with such other information derived from the record to be taken into account at the Advisory Committee. However, the Minister would not be bound to act in accordance with the advice nor were aspects of the committee's dealings be justiciable.[229]

---

[225] [2006] Privy Council's Appeals No. 26 and 37.

[226] [2006] Privy Council's Appeals Nos. 26 and 37.

[227] Ibid.

[228] Chapter V, 'The Executive', *Articles 90-92*, Constitution of the Bahamas (1973).

[229] Reckley v The Minister of Public Safety and Immigration [1995] IAC

Chapter Seven

Diminishing the Death Penalty

'The More Things Change, the More they Remain the Same'

Abolitionist Lordships

What the Privy Council sees in death penalty cases as the unfolding of inalienable human rights, not so apparent at the enactment of the constitution in 1973, others see as privy councillors legislating from the bench and making up the law as they go. It is not the focus of this study to assess the merits of these charges except to address their effect, the placing of limitations on capital punishment within the Caribbean as a part of a global moral initiative under the United Nations Convention on Human Rights.

By its rulings, the Privy Council has effectively diminished the death penalty by addressing a number of contentious matters. These concern mainly the timely administration of justice,[230] the mandatory sentence of death for murder[231] and the prerogative of mercy process in the Bahamas, specifically, and in the Caribbean, generally.[232] Indeed, to

---

13th June 1995).

[230] Hendfield's case 1996
[231] Bowe and Davis Cases 2006
[232] Neville Lewis Case

those contemplating the matter of capital crime, it may seem that the Bahamas and, in a wider context, the Caribbean, are between the devil and the deep blue sea.

The Privy Council, in dealing with the question of the death penalty in the Bahamas, has not challenged its constitutionality per se, since it is expressly provided for in the constitution of the Bahamas in *Article 16(1)*[233] as well as in *Chapter 312* of the Penal Code.[234] Also, they are precluded from doing so due to the 'savings clause' of *Article 17(2)*[235] In Fisher and Woods the *JCPC* reaffirmed its decision from an earlier case that Capital Punishment in the Bahamas is still legal [236] What the Privy Council has done, however, is by its rulings diminish the prospects of carrying out the death penalty in the Commonwealth Caribbean. The study will now consider, in turn, the three mechanisms by which the Privy Council has achieved this.

Administration of Justice

Delays in the administration of justice by the state could amount to cruel and inhuman treatment of death row inmates causing commutation of death sentences to life imprisonment. In *Pratt & Morgan v. The Attorney-General of Jamaica*, the issue of delay in the processing of death penalty cases arose for the first time. [237] In short, their Lordships ruled that any hangings which took place more than five years after sentencing would presume that the delay in carrying out the execution amounted to inhuman and degrading punishment, contrary to *Chapter*

---

[233] Bahamas Constitution (1973)

[234] Statute Laws of the Bahamas

[235] cf. Johanna Harrington, 'The Challenge to the Mandatory Death Penalty in the Commonwealth Caribbean' (2004)98 American Journal of International Law 126.

[236] Fisher and Woods (Bahamas 15October 1998).

[237] [1993] 4 All ER 769.

III section *17* of the Bahamian Constitution.[238] The effect of this ruling was to place the burden ensuring the avoidance of delay upon the State. The ruling in Pratt would significantly affect the legal status of death row inmates across the region, as all sentences of death had to now be reviewed as to their suitability for commutation.[239]

As a direct result, Jamaica would commute 105 sentences of death to life imprisonment, with Trinidad following with 53 and Barbados with 9.[240] Pratt & Morgan was followed in Fisher & Woods and, subsequently, all other death penalty cases in the Bahamas. In *Guerra v Baptiste* the JCPC decided that the 5 year limit handed down in Pratt 'was not intended to provide a yardstick' with which all cases should be judged in constitutional proceedings[241] In *Guerra*, for instance, four years and ten months amounted to cruel and inhumane punishment in contravention of the Constitution of Trinidad and Tobago.[242]

Meanwhile, in *Hendfield v. Attorney-General of the Bahamas*, it was held that a lapse of over three and a half years following sentence of death was enough to warrant inhuman punishment,[243] since, unlike Jamaica, the appeal process is two years and there is no right of appeal to the United Nations.[244] The Judicial Committee of the Privy Council held that the allotted period of time for appeals after a sentence of death in the Bahamas was two years. This would

---

[238] Bahamas Constitution [1973].

[239] Doughterty Chambers report

[240] L.R. Helfer, 'Overlegalising Human Rights: International Relations Theory & The Commonwealth Caribbean Backlash Against Human Rights Regimes' (2002) 102 Columbia Law Review, at 1872).

[241] [1996] App. Case 297.

[242] Ibid.

[243] [1997] (App. Case 413 (P.C. 1996).

[244] Ibid.

provide eighteen (18) months within which appeals to the Privy Council and petitions to international human rights bodies should be completed.[245] This strict timeline to deal with appeals *de jure* and *de facto* before human rights bodies and the Privy Council makes it increasingly challenging for States to carry out capital punishment without serious legal challenge.

Discretion and Death Sentence

By allowing several constitutional challenges to the mandatory death sentence in the Bahamas since Independence in 1973, the Privy Council has substantially diminished the prospects of carrying out the death penalty in the future. The ruling of the *JCPC* on three cases, known as the 'trilogy', involving the Eastern Caribbean Court of Justice forever changed the legal landscape as it relates to capital punishment in the Caribbean. [246] In its ruling, their Lordships stated that the mandatory death penalty amounted to inhuman and degrading treatment in Belize, St. Kitts and St. Lucia.[247] The ruling was upheld in the case of *Lambert and Watson v The Queen* and given effect in Jamaica in 2004.[248]

In addition, the ruling in *Lambert* introduced the element of mitigation by allowing a person under sentence of death to show why, on the facts of the case, including personal background and circumstances, he should not suffer death for the crime committed. [249] Notably, a completely different decision was reached in two similar cases heard by their Lordships with respect to Trinidad and Barbados, namely

---

[245]   cf. *Desmond Baptiste* [2001] 1 AC 1.

[246]   Spence and Hughes v The Queen, *Crim. App. Nos. 20 [1998] & 14 [1997].*

[247]   Ibid.

[248]   Ibid.

[249]   Ibid paragraphs 33-34

Charles Matthew v. The State [250] and *Lennox Ricardo Boyce v. The Queen.* [251]

In these cases it was held that the savings clause of *Sections 6(1)* and *2(6)* of Trinidad and Barbados constitutions, which exempt any laws which were in force before the Constitution from being deemed unconstitutional meant that the mandatory death penalty for murder was constitutional. But, in *Forrester Bowe and Another,*[252] the Privy Council, notwithstanding the savings clause in the Bahamas constitution at *Article 17(2)*[253] and Section 11 of the *Penal Code,* [254] ruled that the mandatory death penalty in the Bahamas and the Caribbean, except for Barbados and the Republic of Trinidad and Tobago, was unconstitutional. The ratio in *Matthew* and *Boyce,* though adverted to, was not applied in *Bowe* and raises the issue of the Privy Council making up the law as they go and cherry picking as they like.

Bowe and *Another* were on death row for eight and six years respectively which, following the rule in *Pratt* and *Hendfield* would exceed the five and three year limit for Jamaica and the Bahamas, respectively, amounting to cruel and inhuman treatment for prisoners incarcerated under sentence of death. In the circumstances the remedy should have been commutation of the sentence of death to life imprisonment rather than a disregard for the savings clause of *Article 17(2).*[255]

---

[250] [2004] UKPC Appeal No. 12 of 2004.
[251] [2004] UKPC Appeal No. 99 of 2004.
[252] *Bowe and Davis[2006]A.C.*
[253] Chapter III, The Bahamas Constitution (1973)
[254] Chapter 84, Statute Laws of The Bahamas (1927)
[255] Bahamas Constituion (1973).

It is also of note that the Privy Council in its ruling in *Matthew* and *Boyce* reversed itself from an earlier decision where it held that the mandatory death penalty was unconstitutional in Trinidad, contending that, in 2004, it was constitutional.[256]

Privy Council's Incongruity

Why this seeming incongruity in the Privy Council's rulings? One response is judicial activism. Also, in its commitment to the abolition movement the Privy Council is inherently at odds with certain provisions of the Bahamian constitution and raises issues about its relevance. In any event, the decision in *Bowe* signalled the end of the mandatory death penalty in the Bahamas.[257] Since 1973, sixteen persons have been executed in the Bahamas, six in the last ten years.[258] Arguably, if the judge had had discretion and mitigating circumstances had been taken into account these persons probably would not have been executed. Thus, by its activism the *JCPC* effectively diminished capital punishment in the Bahamas, perhaps, forever.

Prerogative of Mercy

Article 90 of the Bahamian constitution confers upon the Governor-General a power of pardon.[259] How this power is used in response to death penalty cases has often been hotly debated. Their Lordships have, over the years, altered their views on the topic. In *de Frietas*, an early case, the *JCPC* held that the prerogative of mercy was not justiciable in that 'mercy is not the subject of legal rights;

---

[256] Balkisoon Roodal v. The State [2003] UKPC Appeal No. 18 of 2003.

[257] Doughterty Chambers report

[258] Amnesty International, January 6, 2000.

[259] Bahamas Constitution (1973).

it begins where legal rights end.'[260] This was also the view in *Reckley v. Minister of Public Safety and Immigration* twenty years later.[261]

However, the principle in *de Frietas* and *Reckley* was overturned by the ratio in *Neville Lewis v. Attorney General of Jamaica*,[262] where the *JCPC* held that condemned persons under sentence of death have a right to view material before the committee and should be afforded opportunity to show why their plea for commutation or punishment other than death should be granted. In the landmark ruling of Lewis the Privy Council further diminished the prospects of the death penalty as a viable form of punishment by the state. The ruling opened another door for convicted murderers to make representations of mitigating circumstances, raising the prospects of commutation or pardon.

United Nations Jurisprudence

Two international human rights bodies have further diminished the use of capital punishment in the Bahamas, namely the United Nations Human Rights Committee and the Inter American Commission on Human Rights. They have placed restrictions on the death penalty by a number of Privy Council rulings. In *Baptiste* the Privy Council held that a person under sentence of death has a right to pursue avenues of appeal including any appellate or analogous legal process that is capable of obtaining a reduction or commutation of his or her sentence before the process is rendered nugatory by executive action.[263]

---

[260]   dc Frietas v., Benny et al [1976] AC 239; Judgement delivered 30th April, 1975, at 247).

[261]   [1996] 1 AC 527

[262]   [2000] 3 WLR 1785

[263]   *Desmond Baptiste* [1996] Appeal Case 297.

It, thus, appears that whereas delay in carrying out the death penalty amounts to cruel and inhuman punishment in the rulings of the Privy Council, it does not amount to such in the thinking of the United Nation Human Rights Convention to which the Inter American Convention on Human Rights subscribes.[264] Ironically, they hold that delay in judicial proceedings does not necessarily constitute cruel and inhuman treatment even if it is a source of mental anguish for convicted prisoners. The ratio for promoting this view is that life on death row, harsh as it may be, is still preferable to death.[265]

Further, both human rights bodies have strenuously opposed mercy proceedings which fail to allow convicted persons to participate in the process deciding their fate and the mandatory death penalty, matters which have been resolved by the rulings in *Lewis* and *Bowe* above. They are quick to point out that the mandatory death sentence contravenes the *Article 4(1)* of the Inter American Commission on Human Rights.[266] These human rights bodies are also apt to find that the conditions endured by many death row inmates amount to depressive and terrorizing tactics of the state as was found in a recent case.[267] In that case it was held inmates were not able to sleep or eat, and consequently were deprived of rights guaranteed under *Articles 5(1)* and *(2)* of the convention.[268]

---

[264] *Johnson v. Jamaica*, (Comm. No. 588/1994) UN Document(22.03.1996), at paragraph 8.4.) IACHR view from PC ruling.

[265] Ibid.

[266] Inter American Court of HR, Judgement of 21 June, 2002) Ser. No. 94) CIbid. paras.

[267] Hilaire, Constantine & Benjamin et al v. Trinidad & Tobago (June 21, 2002, Inter American Court of Human Rights, No. 94 (2002).

[268] Ibid. paras153-170.

Again, the Bahamas is not a signatory to the Inter-American Convention on Human Rights. Even if the Bahamas were a signatory to their human rights conventions, it is doubtful whether they would be effective, as unincorporated treaties cannot change domestic law.[269] This is the great principle settled by the civil war and the glorious revolution of the 17th Century.[270] Consequently, human rights provisions have no power unless enacted by the legislature. Until such time Bahamian courts have no power to construe or apply a treaty to extant cases.[271]

Human rights provisions also have no effect upon the rights of citizens in common or statute law, [272] except there is a presumption that either Parliament or the government gives an undertaking that it will not in any way act in a manner to breach its international obligations.[273] In this instance, human rights provisions would have indirect effect upon Bahamian law.

That said, it is unlikely that the Bahamian judiciary would intentionally neglect to consider all the persuasive influence of international human rights conventions in light of evolving *juris* prudence and the Privy Council's recent decisions. Accordingly, notwithstanding the limits placed on the effect of international conventions, they do serve to minimize the use of capital punishment in the Bahamas, if only to delay the carrying out of the death penalty on appeal at human rights bodies.

---

[269] Minister for Immigration and Ethnic Affairs v. Teoh (1995) 183 C.L.R. 273).

[270] Ibid.

[271] J.H. Rayner (Mincing Lane) Ltd. V. Depart ment of Trade & Industry [1990] 2AC 418.

[272] cf. The Parlement Belge (1879) 4 P.D. 129

[273] Minister for Immigration and Ethnic Affairs v. Teoh (1995).

Chapter Eight

Future Relations

'Mending Fences'

The administration of capital punishment in the Bahamas into the future is rife with uncertainty. This is due mainly to the global campaign against the death penalty together with the recent rulings of the Privy Council. Uncertainty with regard to the death penalty is conflated with local politics and the apparent absence of a collective will to produce legislation that will either lead to the abolition of capital punishment or enable it to be enforced with respect to both the rule of law alongside the Constitution and the jurisprudence of the Bahamas.

The core issue is whether to maintain the balance of convenience or to change the status quo regarding the matter of capital punishment verdicts in the Bahamas. Here alternatives to the current state of affairs must be looked at, namely, the Caribbean Court of Justice, a constitutional amendment by a two thirds majority in parliament, a referendum or a compromise with respect to the present arrangement between the Privy Council and the Bahamas, in hopes of resolving the capital punishment debate swirling heedlessly throughout the Bahamas and much of the Caribbean.

Indeed, notwithstanding the lateness of the hour, it is time to mend our fences by focused attention on a cohesive plan of action whose objective should be to exercise intellectuals and the grassroots of society members as to the way forward. Further, it is unclear whether there has been any serious effort to appreciate the role The Caribbean Court of Justice could play in informing the debate. It is clear in the midst of all the uncertainty that the public is overwhelmingly in support of death by hanging for murder convicts.

The Bahamas has at least two readily available options, the approaches adopted by other Caribbean states or the remedies provided in the Privy Council's rulings on the death penalty. Still these approaches and remedies of the respective institutions need to be pitched in a light that is readily understood by the common man who arguably has the greatest stake in the debate. It is time to mend our broken fences in relation to crime and justice issues in the Bahamas by admitting mistakes and seeking to repair collective wrongs perpetrated on society by any number of lapses which have resulted in the status quo.

Caribbean Countries and the Death Penalty

Trinidad, Jamaica and Guyana have employed tactical mechanisms to deal with the death penalty controversy. All three withdrew support for the Inter American Convention on Human Rights and the Optional Protocol to the International Covenant on Civil and Political Rights.[274]

In other cases governments in the Caribbean have neglected to honour appeals before human rights bodies as in the case of Glen Ashby.[275] At the instance of Mr Ashby's hanging,

---

[274] Optional Protocol to the ICCPR, G.A. res. 2200 A (XXI), 21 U.N. GAOR Supplement (N0. 16 at 59, U.N. Doc. A/6316 (1966).
[275] 'Ashby Hanging: An Extrajudicial Killing' by Shelagh Simmons,

an appeal against the dismissal of a constitutional motion was being heard in the Court of Appeal.[276] As such, the appellate process was continuing and an undertaking had been given that the State would not proceed until all avenues of appeal, including to the Judicial Committee of the Privy Council in London, had been exhausted.[277] Interestingly, Trinidad pursued the hanging days before the five year period would have expired, which on the ruling of the Privy Council, would warrant Ashby's commutation.

Other Caribbean States have adopted the tactic of amending their constitutions in an effort to enforce the death penalty in a timely manner as did Barbados on September 2002, perhaps in reply to the ruling of the Eastern Caribbean Court of Appeal questioning the constitutionality of the mandatory death sentence.[278] The amendment provides that 'the imposition of a mandatory sentence of death', along with 'any delay in executing a sentence of death' does not amount to an inconsistency with regards to the contravention of the prohibition on inhuman treatment already found in *section 15(1)* of the Constitution of Barbados.[279] Such strong response to restrictions upon the death penalty by the Barbadian parliament is sweeping in that no hanging had been undertaken since 1984.[280] Barbados further demonstrated its disaffection with the Privy Council when, along with Guyana, it renounced their right to appeal to the Privy Council and signed up instead

---

March 21, 2001, Trinicenter.com

[276] Ibid.

[277] Ibid.

[278] Barbados Constitution, (Amendment) Act 2002-14, Supplement to Official Gazette No. 74 (September 5, 2002), at 216-19.

[279] Ibid.

[280] Joanna Harrington, 'The Challenge to the Mandatory Death Penalty in the Commonwealth Caribbean' (2004) 98 American Journal of International Law 126, p. 139.

to the Caribbean Court of Justice inaugurated in Port of Spain in 2005.[281]

Arguably, Trinidad has exceeded Barbados in its response to impositions on capital punishment in the jurisdiction of the Caribbean, amending its constitution in *Clause 3* to allow executions of persons under sentence of death while they have petitions pending before international human rights bodies.[282] Entrenching itself, Trinidad's amendment provides in *Clause 4* that death row inmates may not be subject to any relief, including a reprieve, until the expiration of at least five years *after* conviction.

The Jamaican Parliament, although not as strenuous in its stance regarding the enforcement of the death penalty have signalled its intention to similarly amend its constitution in response to the Privy Council's death penalty rulings. Their intention can be seen by rejecting a proposal to ban capital punishment in its Parliament which voted 34 to 15 with 10 abstentions to uphold the death penalty.[283] The result of the vote is doubtless linked to the high murder rate in the recent past, 1400 in 2007 and 1671in 2005 with a population of 2.8 million, the same as that of Chicago, where the murder rate in 2007 was low 443.[284]

---

[281] 'Never Before in the History of England: Privy Council Sits Outside Britain,' by Clifford Bishop, July-December, 2007, p. 93, *The Bahamas Investor.*

[282] J. Knowles, 'Capital Punishment in the Commonwealth Caribbean: Colonial Inheritance, Colonial Remedy?', in *Capital Punishment:Strategies for Abolition (2004)* (ed) P. Hodgkinson & W. Schabas, at 306-307.

[283] 'Jamaican Parliament Votes to Keep Death Penalty', November 25, 2008, International Herald Tribune, The Global Edition of the New York Times (The Associated Press).

[284] Ibid.

Some would argue with merit that what is missing in Jamaica, the Bahamas and the Caribbean in contrast to Chicago is the enforcement of the death penalty. Consequently, in the case of Jamaica as in the other mentioned states, there is a commitment at large to resume capital punishment.[285]

The Caribbean pro capital punishment sentiment was evident in the hanging of Charles Elroy La Place in St. Kitts and Nevis in December 2008.[286] The decision to resume hanging in St. Kitts is noteworthy as it was the Eastern Caribbean Court of Appeal, which includes the Kittitian jurisdiction, which ruled in 2001 the mandatory death penalty was unconstitutional.[287] The resumption of hanging could be seen as a direct response of a sovereign Caribbean State to determine its own affairs notwithstanding the rulings of the appeal courts, local and abroad, to restrict the enforcement of capital punishment.

The Caribbean Court of Justice

Of late, the Caribbean Court of Justice has experienced a resurgence of support in light of the controversy surrounding limitations on the enforcement of capital punishment. The Court was formed in the early 1970's when ten nations, Antigua and Barbuda, Barbados, Belize, Grenada, Guyana, Jamaica, St. Kitts and Nevis, St. Lucia, Suriname and Trinidad and Tobago, signed the Agreement Establishing the Caribbean Court of Justice.[288] The establishment of

---

[285]   Ibid.

[286]   'St. Kitts Hangs Man as Islands Revive Death Penalty', by Mike Melia, December 19, 2008, *Associated Press.*

[287]   *Spence and Hughes v. The Queen* (Unreported) 2nd April 2001 (Eastern Caribbean Court of Appeal).

[288]   'The Caribbean Court of Justice: An Overview of the Challenges and Prospects' (28 August 2001), available at http://www.belize.gov. bzfeatures/Caribbean_Court/challenges.

the *CCJ* may constitute the early tactical steps to replace the Judicial Committee of the Privy Council.

A Hanging Court

Some feared the Caribbean Court of Justice would become a hanging court propelling executions in the region.[289] While this may be the fear of some, the many within Caribbean states would welcome a court which would interpret domestic law in a way that would resume capital punishment, in part out of frustration for unabated violence.

By all appearances, the Caribbean Court of Justice cannot in its conduct be justifiably called a 'hanging court', merely accelerating executions in the Caribbean. Despite its late creation, it has demonstrated that it is capable of a *juris prudence* that is intellectually robust and up to the task of adjudicating death penalty cases.

A Competent Court

The legal agility of the *CCJ* is seen in deliberations of the ruling in the Boyce and Joseph and Neville Lewis cases. Lennox Boyce and Jeffery Joseph were in 2001 sentenced to death by hanging for a1999 killing.[290] Their hanging was set for June 2002 but stayed due to an appeal to the Privy Council, at the time the highest appeals court in Barbados, in light of appeals against their sentences to the Inter-American Commission on Human Rights.

---

[289] Amnesty International Report, 'State Killing in the English Speaking Caribbean: A Legacy of Colonial times,' http://www.amnesty.org/library/Index/engAMR050032002.

[290] '*A Landmark Death Penalty Ruling by the Caribbean Court of Justice*', Friday 17 November 2006, www.fidh.org.

In 2005 the Barbados Court of Appeal handed down commutations for both men on the basis that an appeal before the Inter-American Commission on Human Rights would result in the men exceeding the five year limit for carrying out the death penalty.[291] In hearing an appeal on the matter against the Barbados Government, the Caribbean Court of Justice, upheld the Barbados Court of Appeal in relation to the five year doctrine, dispelling again the notion that the court is merely a hanging court.

Again, in *Lewis* the Privy Council ruled that the rulings of the Mercy Committee were now subject to judicial review if it could be demonstrated that they were exercised in a procedurally unfair fashion. In Lewis the Caribbean Court of Justice also considered the weight of petitions of condemned murderers before international human rights bodies.

Coming out of *Lewis* was the issue of the relationship between international conventions entered into by the Executive and domestic law. This issue is clearly linked to murder convict appeals to human rights bodies for relief in their death penalty cases.

The Privy Council ruled in *Lewis* without any clear legal argument that where the Executive signed on to international convention, provisions of the convention assumed the weight of domestic law for the time being. The members of the Caribbean Court of Justice pointed out that such an approach went against the sacred separation of powers principle between the Executive and the Legislature.

A long line of Privy Council authority upheld the tenet that international law cannot become domestic law until the legislature enacts it into domestic law. This safeguard has

---

[291] Ibid.

apparently been eroded in the Lewis ruling of the Privy Council to the Caribbean Court of Justice bewilderment, notwithstanding the Privy Councillors ratio that the ratifying of the international human rights treaty by a Caribbean state meant that its provisions became a part of the state's criminal justice system *pro tem* without a vote by the Legislature.

This meant that no person convicted of murder could be executed before a report by the international human rights body was completed and received by the Mercy Committee based on the 'due process' clause in the Barbados and Trinidad Constitutions. However, when dealing with the same issues in Higgs and Fisher in the Bahamas, the Privy Council ruled that the convicted murderers could be executed as there was a 'protection of the law' clause in the constitution. This double standard was pointed out by the Caribbean Court of Justice in view of the Privy Council's judicial activism at the expense of sound jurisprudence.

It was the Caribbean Court of Justice who, in examining the Privy Council's behaviour, asked how Executive action could magically become a Legislative authority. It also asked how a could a murder convict in Trinidad have a right to appeal to international human rights bodies when those in the Bahamas, Barbados and Jamaica had no right of appeal. In raising these questions, the Caribbean Court of Justice signalled its readiness to robustly adjudicate complex issues surrounding the death penalty requiring rigorous judicial reasoning.

Additionally, in raising its concerns, the Caribbean Court of Justice also demonstrated its judicial temperament by repudiating the Privy Council's reasoning and searching for a legal compromise which would preserve the hallowed doctrine of the separation of powers between the Executive and the Legislature. Accordingly, the Caribbean Court of

Justice, rather than brushing aside the matter, confronted the issue by finding that where a government enters into a human rights treaty in the absence of legislative enactment, a murder convict has an indefeasible legitimate expectation that he would not be executed before his petition was heard.

I contend that this approach is more acceptable than the Privy Council's decision, overruling *Fisher v. Ministry of Public Safety (No. 2)* and *Higgs v. Ministry of National Security*, that the Inter American Human Rights Commission can now become 'legal process' apart from other non-governmental organizations.[292] Again, in arriving at this same conclusion in *Lewis*, the Privy Council has not yet demonstrated how this is done.

By choosing the path of least resistance, the Privy Councillors attempted to justify their position in relation to human rights conventions having effect in domestic law, arguably falling below the standard of what would be expected of the highest appeal court of most Caribbean countries. By holding in Lewis that rights under Inter-American Human Rights Convention are 'mediated' into domestic law through due process thus allowing murderers reasonable time to proceed with their petitions in order for the prerogative of mercy committee could carry out their duty.

Given the creation of the Caribbean Court of Justice and its willingness to engage the death penalty problem, the abolition of capital punishment in the Caribbean will be a challenge for the foreseeable future, the challenges to the mandatory death penalty by the Privy Council notwithstanding.

---

[292] As per Lord Millett's ratio in *Briggs v. Baptiste [2000] 2AC 40* at 54 explaining his decision in *Thomas v. Baptiste [2000] 1 AC.*

Further, given the sovereignty of Independent countries, it is unlikely that Caribbean states will abolish the death penalty any time soon in the face of out of control murder rates and overwhelming public support.[293] Accordingly, the replacing the Judicial Committee of the Privy Council with the Caribbean Court of Justice appears to be an attractive alternative available to Caribbean states.

Regionalism and the Consensus Challenge

It is not clear, however, that all Caribbean states are united in their support for the Caribbean Court of Justice to the extent that they are prepared to abolish the Privy Council as the region's highest appeals court, considering that less than five countries have signed on to the Caribbean court. This suggests that there is latitude for ongoing relations notwithstanding that relations between their Lordships in London and those in the Caribbean have been tested over the controversies surrounding the death penalty. The Privy Council by its own remarks at their historic sitting in The Bahamas are not themselves unmindful of the debate in some cases preferring the Caribbean Court of Justice over their Lordships.[294]

Lord Bingham was of the view that any such decision to abolish the Privy Council as the final appeals court for the Bahamas would rest purely with its citizens as he himself said, speaking on behalf of his peers, 'No one would stop you and no one would wish to do so.'[295] At the same time there is no indication that their Lordships are at any

---

[293] Joanna Harrington, 'The Challenge to the Mandatory Death Penalty in the Commonwealth Caribbean' (2004) 98 *American Journal of International Law* 126, p. 138.

[294] 'Never Before in the History of England: Privy Council Sits Outside Britain,' by Clifford Bishop, July-December, 2007, p. 93, *The Bahamas Investor.*

[295] Ibid.

time soon intending to relinquish their cherished role of being of service to the Bahamas and the Caribbean in the administration of justice. However the issues between the Caribbean states and the Judicial Committee of the Privy Council are resolved it is clear for now that the Caribbean Court of Justice is competent to rule on, *inter alia*, matters which involve the death penalty.

The Abolition Option

The option of abolition is also available to the Bahamas and should be seen as a viable alternative in addressing the capital punishment question. Doubtless, this choice would require a greater degree of the collective will than would be necessary if any of the Caribbean states examples were adopted. But abolition hardly ever comes about in the context of major public opinion or popular support. It is generally achieved through the collective will of the Executive partnering in good faith with the Legislature, who would through time bring along the public.

A goal of the abolitionist is the elimination of the death penalty, sparing convicts from enduring unwarranted suffering. In addressing this issue in *Thomas v. Baptiste*[296] their Lordships thought that it was wrong for a person under sentence of death to have other cruelties added to the manner of his death.[297]

The abolitionist argument is not without merit and as indicated earlier should be properly packaged and set forth in the public domain as a robust and attractive alternative to capital punishment with tangible benefits to the citizenry that can be easily seen.

---

[296] [1999] 3 W.L.R.

[297] 'Ten More Years for Murder Convict' by Tosheena Robinson-Blair, December 4, 2007, *Bahama Journal.*

Restorative Justice

Restorative justice seeks to go beyond the limits of crime and punishment in civil society towards mediation and reconciliation, repairing and restoring relationships of three stakeholders, namely, victims, offenders and their communities. It aims at repairing the harm caused by criminal conduct through cooperative efforts of stakeholders. The process requires an encounter between or among the parties with a view of the offending side taking steps to make amends as regards victims. This is followed by attempts to reintegrate both sides back into society as fully functioning persons with respect to all the circumstances. Some countries even allow the victim to say whether an offender prison term should be shortened or not.

Bahamian society, currently undergoing threats to law and order and fundamental rights of the individual, where seriously contemplated and implemented, could reap considerable benefits from a national reconciliation plan based on principles of restorative justice. Foremost, the plan would have to acknowledge that people most affected by crime should be allowed or enabled to participate in its resolution.

Government's role in the process, as now, would be to maintain good order whereas alongside the collective duty of the community, which would be to promote peace among and between residents regardless of the issues in the case. In this, it is essential that the harm caused by the criminal behaviour be isolated from the offender with a view of repairing or restoring those most affected in the wake of the harm done.

The concept of restorative justice is of value for any number of reasons, one being, it moves us beyond thinking that those who harm others should suffer in isolation. Though 'harm for harm' is important in limiting punishment, a 'tooth for a tooth' will generally not solve crime and punishment problems seeking redress on our doorsteps. This in no way clears the guilty, nor is the argument a way to diminish the integrity of the justice system.

The offender, as much as he or she can, ought to be made accountable in a manner which enables the harm done to be repaired as against more harm being done from a punitive stand point. The process would require direct supervised encounters between and among offenders. Secondary victims such as family and friends affected by the crime as well as family and friends of the offenders should be encouraged to engage in the repair and restoration process.

In certain circumstances, community and government may delegate persons accepted by both sides to help manage goodwill among and between parties. Occasionally, it may be necessary for the government to exercise the option of force for the purpose of maintaining good order. This may be warranted to either preserve or create an atmosphere of civility with a view of enabling resolution of the wrong or harm done to the victim.

In any event, the plan's prospects of success rise or fall on its integrity, legally and morally. Invariably, the plan must include protections for the rights of respective parties, victims and offenders in keeping with prevailing international standards of jurisprudence.

In the end, the idea of restorative justice does not seek to avoid conflict even though a key objective is to achieve peace. The concept embarks on the assumption that the greater the degree of peace in community, the lower will be the incidence of offences against the person originating from within that community. So, in restorative justice, no longer are the two essential parties the government and the defendant but a third party comprised of the victim and the community.

Swift Justice

Swift Justice is an initiative promoted by a number of stake holders comprising the citizenry, judiciary and legislature. It aims to modernize criminal justice services, speed up court cases and improve transparency for a better public understanding of how the legal system works together with local communities in handling minor offenses and persons who perpetrate them. Although it is pitched as an initiative coordinated by the Attorney-General's office, Swift Justice should proceed in lockstep with the judiciary to transmit information in the most efficient manner possible, throughout institutions and agencies of government with the ultimate goal of obtaining justice for victims and their families. This objective is vital to further enable the peaceful enjoyment of the Bahamas for its citizenry.

The success of the initiative would be determined by the level of cooperation among and between judicial institutions, including the police, the probation department, the courts, the prison and the Attorney General's office, and how seamlessly such cooperation could be achieved. Thus, the achievement of swift justice must be a team effort enabling passage of relevant information, without the normal burdens of bureaucracy, from and within government agencies until justice is reached. An essential element of the plan is that serious charges such as murder, armed robbery, rape and other sexual offences be referred directly to the Supreme Court by voluntary bill of indictment. This would fast track grave offences through the legal system, 'leap frogging' them from the information or charge stage, thus, by passing the Magistrate's court and the time consuming delay and avoidance techniques by many lawyers on behalf of the accused.

Weekly or otherwise timely meetings should be agreed upon to lend structure and credibility to the swift initiative plan.

These meetings would enable quality control of procedures that would inevitably be relied upon to maintain the integrity of the plan, such as assurance of forensic evidence in accordance with best practice and legal standards with reference to jurisprudence. Notwithstanding the initiative, more needs to be done as regards witness protection, a vital element of swift justice and its success or failure in the eyes of the public.

Too many instances of serious harm or fatal injury being perpetrated on witnesses have been reported which, if left unchecked, will likely defeat the very purpose of the swift justice initiative. Witnesses should be identified well in advance to trials and guaranteed protection exerting best efforts to safe guard their individual rights and freedoms.

Any swift justice plan should exploit to its fullest modern technology to provide online access of all the laws of the Commonwealth of the Bahamas, updated, so that either at home or at work or in community whoever wishes may readily find laws with their particular matters of interest.

Similarly, virtual courts should be included in the endeavour to allow preliminary hearings to be staged by video when a defendant is held in a police station beyond traditional court hours. Neighbourhood justice panels involving persons from the local community could be established to determine how offenders should make amends for minor criminal breaches. Typically, more than six months pass between an offence taking place and a sentence being handed down, notwithstanding the fact that most matters do not warrant trial or are uncontested.

Clearly, critics of the plan would point to cost and staffing as reasons that would render such a proposal a pragmatic nightmare. However, in this case the means justifies the end of a properly implemented swift justice plan; victims and witnesses get justice sooner than later in which case the focus is taken off the offender and placed where it should be, on the victim.

Again, the concept of swift justice, though promising as a fresh idea inspiring hope for a legal system that needs improvement, it is still not clear in the minds of many what it is in its simplest form. More needs to be done to further explain and simplify the plan. Firstly, the plan should utilize video links for defendants and witnesses appearing in court on a routine basis. This will remove the apprehension many compellable persons have in going to court to literally face the offender. In short, video links would serve to make the process of deposing witnesses less intimidating.

Secondly, the plan should render cases, such as shoplifting, which now take five or more weeks to prosecute, 13 days or less to be dealt with where guilt is admitted and virtual courts are used. Thirdly, the plan should suggest that single magistrates be allowed to sit outside courts, probably in community centres, to dispense justice in low-level, uncontested cases. Fourthly, local magistrates could be given a supervisory role in overseeing the use of summary justice by law enforcement officers or justices of the peace. Fifth, community sentences should be toughened up by introducing a punitive element in every sentence making sense of the punishment. In all this, care would have to be taken that offences are dealt with appropriately in light of justice issues and penalties administered.

Swift justice could also impact positively domestic matters within the Bahamas, since homicide among domestic partners or spouses is notably on the rise. Accordingly, a family mediation system or institution should be established in the Bahamas to mitigate or provide an alternative to divorce and legal separation for the purpose of exploring viable options and remedies as a preventive approach to address the matter of murder in domestic relationships. This program should be properly staffed with competent legal and family advocates gathered from a wide cross section of civil society to reflect a mosaic of religious and ethnic interests in the country.

Although such an institution should produce enforceable agreements with force of law, the process should utilise less formal standards than the courts. Persons who benefit from the service could be referred either by the courts or by other stake holders in society, namely, the church, social service or other entities in society with authority to engage in referrals. Moreover, individuals who themselves sense their need of the intermediary family service should be able throughout a screening procedure to obtain the same.

Next, the family court system could be expanded within its jurisdictional limits to focus on issues affecting local families adversely. Although such a court would be more formal than the family intermediary service aforementioned, it would seek to develop an indigenous jurisprudence that is reflective of matters threatening the civility and survival of the family. It is time for the formulation of a national policy setting forth a family court system with a focus on conflict resolution and prevention through guidance and counselling to help families before their problems result in irreparable breakdown.

This court would focus its resources on filling the gaps and inadequacies of the legal system as it relates to family law in the Bahamas. Other features of this specialized court would include non-adversarial conferences, an alternative dispute resolution support service, such as mediation and counselling, creating a multi-door court system situated within a single facility catering to the unique needs of our archipelago. Government should properly direct itself with urgency to establish such a user friendly family court system which treat the issues which warrant its creation with innovation and pragmatism upholding, at all times, the dignity of the human being and the rule of law.

Chapter Nine

Weighing the Religious Influence

'None is as Blind as He who will not See'

The high percentile of the religious in the Bahamas has led some to infer that the church's view on the issue of capital punishment should not only be sought but followed, pointing to the preamble of the Constitution, that the Bahamas is established upon Christian values, as justification. In treating the matter it may be helpful to assess how the church has behaved in relation to analogous subjects in the not too distant past.

Proposed Amendments

Arguably, the proposed amendments to the *Sexual Offences and Domestic Violence Act (1991)*, also commonly known as the 'marital rape law', constitute a fitting example which demonstrates the mindset of religious bodies, some would say, to progressive ideas of a postmodern era in the Bahamas. The issue then was, and still is, whether a spouse within a properly constituted marriage could be guilty of rape as an offence punishable by law. In 2009, the year parliament introduced the Bill to amend the Act; religious entities galvanized to effectively kill any prospects of the legislature succeeding at enactments to change the existing law which perpetuates discrimination against women in marriage.

Received Wisdom

I contend that the religious side proceeded to promote then its position against amending the Act without any or any careful treatment of the issue from either a biblical, social or legal perspective as it is seemingly at ease doing with the issue of capital punishment and the death penalty. In the Old Testament, the death penalty was warranted in cases of rape. In Deuteronomy 22:25-28 it states that 'If a man finds a girl who is engaged and the man forces her and lies with her, then only the man who lies with her shall die.' This passage signifies the weight of an offence of rape against the virtue and dignity of a woman, intimating categorically that significant harm perpetrated by sexual act upon a female ought not to be tolerated in any relationship by any civil or religious body in society.

Rape is defined under the Sexual Offences and Domestic Violence Act as: 'An act of any person not under 14 years of age having sexual intercourse with another person who is not his spouse without consent, without consent being extorted by fears, threats or fear of bodily harm; with consent obtained by personating the spouse of that other person, or with consent obtained by false and fraudulent representations as to the nature and quality of the act.' An indictable offence, Section 6(1) provides that the penalty for rape is life imprisonment or 7 years for the first offence and 14 years for the second. In the main, the amendment sought to delete the words 'who is not his spouse,' in essence making it illegal for any person to have sex with another without consent, regardless as to whether they are married or not. It was the mistaken view of not a few that the matter would have attracted the full and unequivocal support of the church which, regrettably, it did not.

Privilege Misinterpreted

Back to the question, 'Can a spouse within marriage be found guilty of rape as an offence punishable by law?' Both in my view and the jurisprudence throughout the Commonwealth of Nations, the answer is clearly, yes. However, the church in the Bahamas said, no. Some point to St. Paul in 1Corinthians 7:3-5 where he says, 'Let the husband render to his wife the affection or benevolence due her, and likewise also the wife to her husband. The wife does not have authority over her own body, but the husband does.' Those who use the Pauline injunction, to promote male headship in marriage to the detriment of a woman's rights in marriage, are either unaware or impervious to civil and legislative progress made on the topic over time.

Undeniable Progress

Even though Paul's statement served as the foundation of the Common Law, in both the United States and the United Kingdom for hundreds of years, these jurisdictions have expanded their interpretation on marriage to say that marital rape is a reality vis-à-vis domestic violence and should now be criminalized. Obviously, this position was not arrived at easily or overnight and warrants an appreciation of the historical developments.

As far back as 1736, noted jurist, Sir Matthew Hale, held that rape was impossible in marriage and could not be recognized since a wife would have given herself to her husband in a manner which she could not retract. This ruling provides the basis for what is widely referred to as the exemption for rape in marriage. Remarkably, since then a number of things have changed. The case of R v Clarke [1949] 2 ALL ER 448 marks the first time rape by a husband was prosecuted in England. In this case the court refused to allow the marital exemption. Again, in

R v O'Brien [1974] 3 ALL ER 663 the court held that no exemption should be allowed after the Decree Nisi in divorce proceedings.

In 1975 the United States took the first step toward removing the marital rape exemption. However, it was not until 1993, eighteen years after, that the exemption for marital rape was entirely abolished in the United States of America. It should be noted here that the United Kingdom led the way on the issue by abolishing the marital rape exemption in 1991, two years ahead of the United States when, in R v Kowalski (1988) 86 Cr App. R. 339, R v J [1991] and R v Sharples [1960] Crim. LR 198, the House of Lords abolished exemption all together and convicted husbands of assault and indecent assault, respectively.

Marital Rights Qualified

Meanwhile, human rights in marriage took a foothold, casting doubt on the belief that marital right to intercourse was absolute as was argued in the case of R v R [1992] 1 AC 599 (p. 3) in the England. By 1997 seventeen nations had enacted laws which made rape in marriage a crime. This figure increased to 50 by 2003 and 104 by 2006. In 2006, a minority of four nations held that marital rape was only a criminal offence where spouses were judicially separated. Currently, the Bahamas falls within this group. In its 2008 Human Rights report the United Nations noted that while rape is considered illegal in the Bahamas, the law does not address spousal rape. As such sexual violence within a marriage continues widespread and unabated by law.

Unintended Consequences

Aiding and abetting this inequity in marriage and gender prejudice are religious advocates who contend, to allow the cited amendments to the Act would make husbands potential rapists, contradicting the sacrament of marriage. In an attempt to support their claim, some stridently argue that a man cannot rape his wife when the Bible states that she should submit herself to him. But what happens if a wife does not consent to intercourse? Should her rights be extinguished or suspended to facilitate the forceful advances of her husband? Further, why do uninvited sexual acts of force perpetrated on a woman outside of marriage amount to criminal offences whereas, the same acts, within marriage do not? Prima facie, if rape is wrong outside of marriage, it stands to reason that it is wrong within marriage. If it is a criminal offence outside of marriage, in keeping with the tenets of Natural Justice, it should constitute a crime within marriage. In all fairness, something clearly inequitable with the status quo, yet religious advocates uphold it nevertheless, belittling the common good. By their antagonism to amendments that could right this wrong they have caused legislators to cower.

Separation of Roles

In the circumstances, I prefer to speak of a separation of roles as opposed to a separation of church and state, simply because my view is that such a distinction is mistaken and untenable in the Bahamas. Although it is not our focus here, I offer brief comment on the authority of the church and the branches of government to address issues of import relative to the inalienable rights of the individual, their peaceful enjoyment of the Bahamas as a sovereign people in their pursuit of happiness. Neither should seek, in the discharge of their duties, to unduly influence the other. In short, churches should not seek to run the government as the government should not seek to run churches. Put another way, just as it would be absurd for Members of Parliament to all of a sudden assume pastoral leadership of the church it would be similarly absurd for Pastors to suddenly seize control of the legislature, yet each has legitimacy in their respective settings to manage and govern the affairs of the bodies from which they derive their authority.

Accordingly, the church should be measured in its counsel to the state as well as the state should not embark on governance subject to the wishes of the church. Indeed, church and state should ever be kept separate notwithstanding that they ought to peacefully co-exist in a state that is cooperative. The purpose of laying the case of marital rape, then, was to demonstrate how religious advocates, though well meaning, may at times stand in the way of progress in civil society. This suggests that those in whom the confidence of the citizenry is reposed, namely, the executive, the legislature and the judiciary should be careful not to rely too heavily or inappropriately on the faith community to resolve issues concerning the inalienable rights and freedoms of the individual. Perhaps too, this prescription should be applied in dealing with the matter of capital punishment. The state, while respectfully listening to the church, should not rely on the church, as it did on the issue of marital rape, to determine the way forward on an issue of such moment as the death penalty and capital punishment.

Chapter Ten

Implications

'Uneasy Lies the Head that Wears the Crown'

At present a stalemate exists between rulings of the Privy Council and the Bahamas. The matter of capital punishment creates a legal jeopardy where the Judges in adjudicating death penalty cases seem damned if they do and damned if they do not. The status quo exerts undue pressure on jurists bound by oath to properly interpret and apply the law in harmony with the Constitution of the Bahamas to ensure that the rights and freedoms of its citizens and those domiciled in its jurisdiction are protected.

The conflict lies between the rulings of the Privy Council and the provisions of the Constitution regarding the death penalty. Even though the Privy Council's ruling in 2006 that the mandatory death penalty for the crime of murder is unconstitutional and, thus, abolished, the ruling does nothing to resolve the issue of capital punishment other than place it within the discretion of Supreme Court Judges.

It is yet to be seen whether rulings calling for the death penalty on discretionary grounds will stand up to the Privy Council. Even if the discretionary death penalty stood on appeal it is unlikely that such appeal would be processed within the five year period in *Pratt and Morgan* for Jamaica or three and a half year limit in Hendfied for the Bahamas, given the delays inherent in the judicial system and the Privy Council's abolitionist stance.

The Bahamas could elect to adopt the approach of Barbados and Trinidad by amending its constitution to guarantee that the laws of the land and the judicature would not be thwarted by outside forces. Such a position would have to be weighed against the global abolition movement which is becoming increasingly difficult to rebut. The more countries pursue capital punishment in their jurisdiction the more they are isolated in the global environment. However, some would argue that Caribbean states are encouraged in their path of self determination in keeping with the notion of regionalism which, though not addressed in the study, has its own merits.

To say the least, the existing climate of uncertainty undermines the rule of law. When this occurs respect for the laws of the land are diminished, and if left unchecked regard for lawgivers will be eroded, the result of which creates a spawning bed for incidences of vigilantism and anarchy where a lack of confidence in the justice system will likely incite persons to take the law into their own hands to be the judges in their own causes. Unabated, this vacuous state of jurisprudence will impliedly affect the quality of the nation's existence as a sovereign and Independent state.

Therefore, the findings of the study suggest that the suspension or abolition of the death penalty, though rife with challenges, constitutes the better way forward in achieving the aims of justice and the rule of law. This approach offers good prospects of success that would hopefully cure the inertia plaguing the machinery of justice to regain the elements of certainty, clarity and predictability which are the touchstones of any effective legal system, currently at risk because of the whirling controversy surrounding the death penalty.

Clearly, based on the posture of the judiciary and the legislature, it is unlikely that death sentences will be carried out again in the Commonwealth of the Bahamas. In this matter, the Bahamas is not alone as the entire Caribbean faces similar challenges alongside the capital punishment debate, equally frustrated their citizenry in wake of escalating homicides in the respective states.

At the heart of the debate is the perception by the citizenry that either the state is impotent to govern as regards the problem or the judiciary, given the rulings of the Privy Council on the death penalty, are prevented from applying the laws of the land. Either Capital punishment should be allowed to proceed or the law should be changed, by parliament or by referendum. This would reclaim loss degrees of credibility in the rule of law in the Bahamas which will, in turn, enable certitude, an essential outcome of any worthwhile jurisprudential endeavour. In helping to achieve this, the Executive ought to engage the Official Opposition in a strategic alliance to ensure that best efforts are brought to bear on the problem at hand. That said, the moratorium on capital punishment in the Commonwealth of the Bahamas seems more the creation of the Privy Council and their abolitionist mindset than any challenge posed by the constitutionality of the death penalty.

Despite attempts by the Privy Council, Inter-American Human Rights Commission and the Organization of American States capital punishment, remains the law of the land. In the circumstances, it can either be abolished by enactments of Parliament, an amendment to the constitution of the Bahamas or rulings from the Judiciary. Meanwhile, the moratorium on capital punishment in the Bahamas indicates that abolition is on the way. Arguably, it is currently *de facto* and to a considerable degree *de jure*. Abolition, to be of any merit, must in the final analysis be of lasting benefit to the citizenry generally as opposed to particular special interests or vested stakeholders in the debate. If used for the purposes of sorting out our jurisprudential differences on both sides of the Atlantic, for the enhancement and wellbeing of Bahamians, every effort should be exerted to resolve the issue once and for all. In all of this, stakeholders must be forever cautious, in treating the subject, to avoid being ensnared by the prevailing cultural, religious and political influences of the day, with a view and collective will to what will benefit the citizenry in perpetuity.

Bibliography

CASES

BALKISSOON ROODAL v. THE STATE [2003] *UKPC* Appeal No. 18 of 2003.

Bowe and Another, P.C. 8March 2006, [2006]1WLR 1623.

BRIGGS V. BAPTISTE [2000] 2AC 40.

CHARLES MATTHEW V. THE STATE [2004] UKPC APPEAL No. 12 of 2004.

De Frietas v. Benny et al [1976] *AC* 239; Judgement delivered 30th April, 1975, at 247.

COUNCIL OF CIVIL SERVICE UNIONS V. MINISTER FOR CIVIL SERVICE (E.H.R.L.R. 156). (February 6, 1996). *Times.*

Desmond Baptiste [2001] 1 AC 1.

Desmond Baptiste [1996] Appeal Case 297.

FISHER V. MINISTRY OF NATIONAL SECURITY P.C. [1992]2WLR 349; [2000] 1A.C. 434).

Furman v. Georgia 408 U.S. 238 (1972) United States Supreme Court Case.

GREGG V. GEORGIA 428, U.S. 153, 185-186 *(1976).*

GUERRA V. BAPTISTE [1996] App. Case 297.

HENDFIELD AND OTHERS V. MINISTER OF NATIONAL SECURITY P.C. 1996. [1997] (App. Case 413).

HILAIRE, CONSTANTINE & BENJAMIN ET AL V. TRINIDAD & TOBAGO (June 21, 2002). *Inter American Court of Human Rights, No. 94 (2002).*

INTER AMERICAN COURT OF HUMAN RIGHTS JUDGEMENT. (June, 2002). Ser. No. 94.

INTER AMERICAN COMMISSION ON HUMAN RIGHTS Reso. 33/88, Case 9786 (Peru) in OEA/Ser. L/VII, 76 December 10, 18, September 1989.

J. H. RAYNER (MINCING LANE) LTD. V. DEPART MENT OF TRADE & INDUSTRY [1990] 2AC 418.

JOHNSON V. JAMAICA (Comm. No. 588/1994) UN Document(22.03.1996) at paragraph 8.4.) IACHR.

JOHN JUNIOR HIGGS AND DAVID MITCHEL V. THE MINISTER OF NATIONAL SECURITY [2000] PC Appeal No. 45 of 1999.

LAMBERT AND WATSON V. THE QUEEN [2004] UKPC App. Case No. 36 of 2003.

LARRY JONES V. THE ATTORNEY GENERAL OF THE COMMONWEALTH OF THE BAHAMAS 1995 [2006] Privy Council's Appeals No. 26 and 37.

LENNOX RICARDO BOYCE V. THE QUEEN [2004] UKPC Appeal No. 99 of 2004.

MINISTER FOR IMMIGRATION AND ETHNIC AFFAIRS V. TEOH (1995) 183 C.L.R. 273).

NEVILLE LEWIS AND OTHERS V. ATTORNEY GENERAL OF JAMAICA [2000] 3WLR 178).

PRATT AND MORGAN V. THE ATTORNEY GENERAL OF JAMAICA [1993] 4 ALL ER 769.

PRIVY COUNCIL (October 5, 1998). [1999]2 WLR 349; [2000] *1A.C.* 434).

RECKLEY V. THE MINISTER OF PUBLIC SAFETY AND IMMIGRATION [1995] 1 AC 13 June 1995.

SPENCE AND HUGHES V THE QUEEN, CRIMINAL APPEAL. (Nos. 20). [1998] & 14 [1997]. (Judgment given 2 April 2001). (Eastern Caribbean).

THE PARLEMENT BELGE (1879) 4 P.D. 129

2WLR 281 [1996] A.C. 527. [1996]. (February 6, 1996). *Times.*

STATUTES/GOVERNMENT PUBLICATIONS

BARBADOS CONSTITUTION (AMENDMENT) ACT 2002-14. (September 5, 2002). Supplement to Official Gazette No. 74, at 216-19.

DEPARTMENT OF YOUTH, MINISTRY OF YOUTH (2008), *Bahamas Government.*

MAYNARD-GIBSON, ALLYSON. (May 17, 2006). Remarks on Swift Justice. Paper presented at a meeting of The Honourable Attorney General and Minister of Legal Affairs at a Press Conference, Nassau, Bahamas.

PARLIAMENTARY POWERS. *Bahamas Constitution 1973, Article 54, Chapter V.*

ROYAL BAHAMAS POLICE FORCE (2008). Detected Crimes-All Bahamas: 1963-2005. Nassau, Bahamas: Author.

STATES WITHOUT THE DEATH PENALTY AND MURDER RATES. (June 27, 2008). *Death Penalty Information Centre.*

THE BAHAMAS. (19June 2008). *The World Fact Book. Central Intelligence, USA.*

THE BAHAMAS CONSTITUTION: OPTIONS FOR CHANGE. *(2003).* The Bahamas Constitutional Commission. *Commission.Secretariat, Government of the Bahamas Printing Department, Nassau, Bahamas.*p. 4.

UN GENERAL ASSEMBLY. (December 18, 2007). Resolution GA/10678 at the 62nd Plenary Session, New York, USA.

UN HIGH COMMISSION ON HUMAN RIGHTS REPORT 1999/61 of 58th meeting. (April 1999).

UPDATED PROTOCOL, CARIBBEAN COURT OF JUSTICE. (April 17, 2000). *Caribbean Community Secretariat.*

ARTICLES

ADAMS, DAVID.*(2002, December 4)* Jamaica to Bring Back Hanging in Drug Crime Fight. *TIMES (London).*

BROWN, ARTESIA. (November 12, 2008). God Alone Can Enforce the Death Penalty. *The Nassau Guardian.*

CAPITAL PUNISHMENT. (December 7, 1998). *The Evening (Standard)Bahama Journal.*

BROWN, THOMAS. (December 10, 2007). Nation Sowed Seeds of Crime. *The Nassau Guardian*

DAMES, CANDIA. (January 14, 2009). Crime Council Wants Hanging. *The Nassau Guardian.*

DAMES, CANDIA. Crime Commission Member Wants Capital Punishment Abolished. (December 2008). *The Nassau Guardian.*

DAMES, CANDIA. (March 12, 2004). Murderers Still Awaiting Review of Death Sentences. *The Bahama Journal.*

DAMES, CANDIA. (May 8, 2008). Prime Minister: Case Could Answer Capital Punishment Question. *Bahama Journal.*

DAVIS, ARTESIA AND ST. ROSE, SAMORA. (April 9, 1996) Panel Split on Capital Punishment. *Nassau Guardian.*

DAVIS, ARTESIA. Court of Appeal Upholds Tido Death Sentence. (October 17, 2008). *The Nassau Guardian.*

GAIL, STEPHEN. (January 21, 2006). Religious and Community Leaders On Capital Punishment. *The Bahama Journal.*

KEEPING DEATH PENALTY WILL NOT CUT MURDER RATES. (December 2, 2008). *Jamaican Gleaner News.*

FOULKES, SIR ARTHUR. (May 12, 2006). Privy Council Rules on Bahamas Death Penalty Issues. *Bahama Pundit.*

GAY, STEPHEN. RELIGIOUS AND COMMUNITY LEADERS ON CAPITAL PUNISHMENT. (January 2006). *Bahama Journal.*

JAMAICAN PARLIAMENT VOTES TO KEEP DEATH PENALTY. (November 25, 2008). *International Herald Tribune, The Global Edition of the New York Times (The Associated Press)*.

LUNDY, TAMEKA. (February 4, 2008). Death Penalty Row Deepens. *Bahama Journal*.

MCKENZIE, TAMARA. National Mean Grade. (August 30, 2003). *Nassau Guardian*.

MELIA, MIKE. (December 19, 2008). St. Kitts Hangs Man as Islands Revive Death Penalty. *Associated Press*.

MINNIS, KARAN. (November 15, 2007). To Hang or Not to Hang is the Swinging Question. *The Nassau Guardian*.

MURDERERS STILL AWAITING REVIEW OF DEATH SENTENCES. (June 3, 2008). *Bahama Journal*.

NEW JERSEY ABOLISHES DEATH PENALTY. (December 17, 2007). Available at http://www.*National Public Radio*. NPR.org. Accessed on 4 February 2009.

OUTTEN, LA SHONNE. (March 25, 2006). Killers Spared Hanging. *The Nassau Guardian*.

PM: HEADS OF GOVERNMENT SUMMIT SPEECH. (July 1, 1999). *Bahama Journal*.

PRIVY COUNCIL (Ja). (November 4, 1993). *Times*.

ROBERTSON, JESSICA. (March 13, 1996). Reckley Hanged. *The Tribune*.

ROBINSON-BLAIR, TOSHEENA. (December 4, 2007). Ten More Years For Murder Convict. *The Bahama Journal*.

ROLLE, KRYSTEL. Boyd to Uphold Church's Stand on Homosexuality. (January 1, 2009). *The Nassau Guardian.*

ROLLE, KRYSTAL (June 10, 2008).Turnquest:National Security a Priority. *The Nassau Guardian.*

ROLLE, KRYSTEL. (October 21, 2008). Crime Rate Up 14 Percent. *The Nassau Guardian.*

SMITH, IANTHIA. (March 25, 2006). Crime Wave Concerns All. *Nassau Guardian.*

SMITH, IANTHIA. (April, 2006). D-Day on Death Row. *The Nassau Guardian.*

SMITH, LARRY. (March 15, 2006). Capital Punishment in The Bahamas. *Bahama Journal.*

SMITH, LARRY. (April 12, 2006). Capital Punishment in The Bahamas. *Bahama Pundit.*

SMITH, LARRY. (June 22, 2008). Former Police Prosecutor Warns of Judicial Collapse in the Bahamas. *Bahama Journal.*

SUNSTEIN, CASS R. AND WOLFERS, JUSTIN. (June 30, 2008). A Death Penalty Puzzle: The Murky Evidence For and Against Deterrence. page A-11, *Washington Post.*

THOMPSON, JOHN. (January 30, 1998). Crime in the Bahamas. *BBC News.*

THURSTON, GLADSTONE. (May 7, 1996). Reinstating Capital Punishment for Convicted Murderers. *Nassau Guardian.*

WELLS, ERICA. (January 18, 2006). Prison Security in Question. *The Bahama Journal*

WELLS, ERICA. Corporal Law in the Bahamas to be Repealed. (November 8, 2008). *The Nassau Guardian.*

WORLD: AMERICAS TWO EXECUTED IN BAHAMAS. (October 15, 1998). *BBC News.*

JOURNALS

BAILEY, WILLIAM AND PETERSON, RUTH. (1997). Murder, Capital Punishment, and Deterrence: A Review of the literature. In Hugo Bedau. (ed). *The Death Penalty In America: Current Controversies.* New York: Oxford University Press.

BISHOP, CLIFFORD. (July-December 2007). Never Before in the History of England: Privy Council Sits Outside Britain. *The Bahamas Investor* (Vol. 2, p. 93).

BOWERS, WILLIAM J. & PIERCE, GLENN. (1980). Deterrence or Brutalization: What is the Effect of Execution? (26) *453, 456. Crime & Delinquency.*

EHRLICH & GIBBONS. (1977). On the Measurement of the Deterrent Effect of Capital Punishment and the Theory of Deterrence. (6) 35. *Journal of Legal Studies.*

EHRLICH, ISAAC. (1975). The Deterrent Effect of Capital Punishment: A Question of Life and Death. 65 *Am. Econ. Rev.* 397, 415-16.

HARRINGTON, JOHANNA. (2004) The Challenge to the Mandatory Death Penalty in the Commonwealth Caribbean. (98)126. *American Journal of International Law.*

HELFER, L.R. (2002). Overlegalising Human Rights: International Relations Theory & The Commonwealth

Caribbean Backlash Against Human Rights Regimes. 102 *Columbia Law Review,* at 1872.

HESSING, DICK J., DE KEIJSER, JAN W., AND ELFFERS, HENK. (December 2003). Explaining Capital Punishment Support in an Abolitionist Country: The Case of the Netherlands. *Law and Human Behaviour,* 27(6), *p. 605-622.*

HODGEKINSON, P. AND RUTHERFORD, A. (EDS). Capital Punishment in Global Perspective. Winchester Waterside Press. *British Journal of Criminology (2005) 45(3), 402-406.*

JOHNSON, SCOTT L. THE BIBLE AND THE DEATH PENALTY: IMPLICATIONS FOR CRIMINAL JUSTICE EDUCATION. (Spring 2000). *Journal of Criminal Justice Education. 11(1), p. 18.*

SELLIN, THORSTEN (1959) The Death Penalty. *American Law Institute, Philadelphia,* p. 34.

SHEPHERD, JOANNA. (June 2004). Murders of Passion, Execution Delays, and the Deterrence of Capital Punishment. *Journal of Legal Studies.*

SHORANI, M. 'A Journey of Two Countries: A Comparative Study of The Death Penalty in Israel and South Africa.' (2001) 24 *Hastings International & Contemporary Law Review.*

SHEPHERD, JOANNA. *(June 2004).* Murders of Passion, Execution Delays, and the Deterrence of Capital Punishment. *Journal of Legal Studies.*

SMITH, LARRY. Rethinking the Death Penalty. (June 29, 2008). *The New Black Magazine.*

WEBSITES

A LANDMARK DEATH PENALTY RULING BY THE CARIBBEAN COURT OF JUSTICE. November 17, 2006. Available at *http:// www.fidh.org.* Accessed 6 February 2009

AMNESTY INTERNATIONAL REPORT. (2002). State Killing in the English Speaking Caribbean: A Legacy of Colonial times. Accessed 6February 2009. Available at *http:// www. amnesty. org/library/Index/ eng AM R050032002.*

AMNESTY INTERNATIONAL WEBSITE. Available at *http://Web.amnesty.org/web.nsf/print/death penaltycountries eng.* Accessed 6 January 2000.

CAPITAL PUNISHMENT AND DETERRENCE. Available at http//*www 1bptbridgepor.edu/—darmri/capital.html.* Retrieved 9 January 2009

CAPITAL PUNISHMENT. Available at http ://www. answers. com/ topic/capital- punishment. Accessed 4February 2009.

DAVIS, ARTESIA. Murder Trial Delayed. Available at *http://* www.the Nassau guardian. net/ national_local. Accessed 26 February 2009.

DOES CAPITAL PUNISHMENT DETER CRIME? Available at *http://www.enotes.com/does-capital- article//print.* Accessed 1January 2009.

INTER AMERICAN COMMITTEE ON HUMAN RIGHTS. Available at http:// *OAS Website.* Accessed 5 January 2009.

SHAPIRO, WALTER. What Say Should Victims Have? Available at http://*www.cap.org.askJeeves.com*. Accessed 29 April 2009.

SHEPHERD, JOANNA. Capital Crimes and Retribution. Available at http://*www.Michigan Law Review.org/ archive/104/2/Shepherd*. Accessed 6 January 2009.

SIMMONS, SHELAGH. Ashby 21 March 2001Hanging: An Extrajudicial Killing. Available at **Error! Hyperlink reference not valid.** Trinicenter.com. Accessed 4February 2009.

VAN DEN HAAG, ERNEST. On Deterrence and the Death Penalty. Available at http://*www.public. ia state.edu/—cfehr*. Accessed 6January 2009.

THE CARIBBEAN COURT OF JUSTICE: AN OVERVIEW OF THE CHALLENGES AND PROSPECTS—28 August 2001. Available at http:// *www. belize. Gov.bzfeatures / Caribbean_Court. Challenges*. Accessed 4February 2009.

THE BAHAMAS DEATH PENALTY HANDED DOWN IN HISTORIC SENTENCING. Available at http://www handsoffcain. info/archivio_news/200604.php. Accessed 15January 2009.

PRIVY COUNCIL TO RULE ON DEATH PENALTY: March 2004. Available at http://www.*Caribbean Net News*. Accessed on 25th January 2009.

BOOKS

CATECHISM OF THE CATHOLIC CHURCH (1988) Number 2267, Part Three, Section 2, chapter 2 and *The Lambeth Conference.*

COFFEY, JOHN MOTT. New Suspect Charged in Brewer Case. (February 8, 2008). *Commercial Dispatch Bureau.*

INTERPRETER'S BIBLE 1952; Mercer Dictionary of the Bible; Anchor Bible Dictionary

RICHARDSON, P.J. (ED). (2009). *Archbold: Criminal Pleading, Evidence and Practice.* U.K: Sweet & Maxwell: Thompson Reuters.